A PLACE CALLED
Common Sense

(GOD'S WORD IN A SECULAR WORLD)

Written by:
REGINA STONE MATTHEWS

Illustrated by:
DONNA BROWN

No part of this book may be reproduced or transmitted in any form or by any means electronic or mechanical, including photocopying and recording, or by any information storage or retrieval systems, without permission in writing from the author. The only exception is by a reviewer, who may quote short excerpts in review.

Copyright © 2019 by Regina Stone Matthews
All rights reserved.
www.reginamatthews.com
Atwater & Bradley Publishers
ISBN: 978-1-7332127-4-8

All Scripture quotations, unless otherwise indicated are taken from the Holy Bible, New International Version®, NIV® Copyright ©1973, 1978, 1984, 2011 by Biblica, Inc.® Used by permission. All rights reserved worldwide.

For my children and my grandchildren. You are that extra beat in my heart, that extra spring in my step. Show others what you've always shown me and that's your excellence. Go out into the world and let them know you are Christians by your love.
You are the future.

I love you to the moon and back.

Contents

Acknowledgment vii

Introduction ix

Chapter One 1
A Clique-Click Is Not Only the Sound a Gun Makes, But It's Just as Deadly

Chapter Two 9
Beware of the Trojan Horse

Chapter Three 15
Corporate Gentleman or Corporate Cad?

Chapter Four 21
Crazy Old People

Chapter Five 27
Doc Baker Never Asked for Money Up Front

Chapter Six 34
Finding Your Emotional Intelligence

Chapter Seven 44
Hanging on To Bad Messages

Chapter Eight 51
I've Seen Hell and I Don't Want to Go There!

Chapter Nine 59
Just How Much Are You Invested in Your Decision?

Chapter Ten 68
Lowering of the Bar

Chapter Eleven 77
Never Judge a Book by Its Cover

Chapter Twelve..83
So, Are You Having Fun in Your Pursuit of Happiness?
That's the Question

Chapter Thirteen 91
Standing in the Shadow of Rocky Balboa

Chapter Fourteen... 101
The Ways and Means of Atticus Finch

Chapter Fifteen 111
What in the World is Stone Soup?

Chapter Sixteen... 119
When Leaders Emerge

Chapter Seventeen 128
When Sense and Sensibility Left the Building

Chapter Eighteen... 137
Will the Real Towanda Please Stand Up?

Chapter Nineteen 144
Where Have You Been All My Life Michael Buble?

Chapter Twenty 151
Dear Mother, Remember the time you said you wanted to go to sleep one night and wake up in heaven?
I thought you were just kidding.

Postscript.. 157

Epilogue 158

Acknowledgment

To my Lord and Savior Jesus Christ, without whom I would be nothing. May my words glorify Your name. May my actions make You proud. May I do the work that advances Your kingdom.

To my family. My husband, David. My daughters, Sandi, Noel, and Ashlee. My sons-in-law, Tim, Jeremie, and Kevin. My grandchildren, Danielle, Skye, Dylan, Haylie, and Finley. I love you all beyond measure.

To my parents, Claude and Evelyn Stone, who gave me life, who loved me, and who raised me to be the best person I could be. I miss you each and every day. I love you dearly.

To my super talented illustrator, Donna Brown, whose support and patience is never-ending and forever appreciated. Thank you, my dear friend.

To my editor, Anne Mateer, a gifted writer and editor. I cherish your guidance and your patience. Thank you, my dear friend.

Psalm 139:1–5

Introduction

God's Word.
   The Bible.
   Is it just a collection of made-up stories?
Or
Is it divine inspiration?
How many books are in the Bible?
How many authors contributed to the Bible?
Over how many years?
What year did the first writings occur?

If the Bible has 66 books, written by 39-40 authors, over a period of 1,500 years, possibly beginning 3,500 years ago—how exactly is any of it relevant?

And, if like "they" say, Moses wrote the first five books, and he lived between 1500 and 1300 BC, how then can we even take what's written in those first five books and apply it to today's world? Plus, this guy wrote about things that happened long before he was ever born. How does that work?

Let's put a stumbling block into everything by adding one more bit of info. A lot of this stuff wasn't even written down. Generation after generation simply spoke the words. They passed them down through various verbal communications. How reliable is that? Then something like 500 years of total silence passed—no contributions toward the Bible whatsoever.

So, we have this really old book that may or may not have been written by whom exactly? Divine men? Guys who just wanted to get some things off their chest?

I ask this question: When reading the Bible, how important

is it *when* the Bible was written? Some might say the *when* part is very important. As for me, I say it's not at all. I say, it's more important *what's* written—the words, if you will.

I also submit that those 39-40 authors were clearly inspired by God. Take a look at the book of Second Timothy. Specifically, 2 Timothy 3:16. Here's how it reads: "All Scripture is breathed out by God and profitable for teaching, for reproof, for correction, and for training in righteousness," Pay particular attention to the words "All Scripture is breathed out by God." These authors wrote in their own style, voice, personality, but they each wrote exactly what God intended.

In *A Place Called Common Sense: God's Word in a Secular World*, I hope to prove that the Bible most assuredly applies in today's world. Our world's events are intricately woven throughout the Bible—yesterday's, today's, and tomorrow's.

How do I know all this you might ask? Well, it's all a matter of common sense.

Let's take a walk together through some of the topics that we read about or hear about daily and I'll show you how God's Word fits right into each of those topics. Like my previous book, *Anyone Seen My Rose-colored Glasses?: God's Word in Everyday Life,* if you're wearing those rose-colored glasses, you'll miss out on a whole lotta fun. God's Word fits right in with all our everyday occurrences. You know the ones. The things that we personally deal with on a daily basis.

Likewise, if you're living in a place called folly, you'll have a hard time finding your way to that place called common sense. Are you game to journey with me? I promise it won't hurt a bit. In fact, I bet you'll come out the winner. Take a chance. You just might be the better for it. You don't want me to pull out the triple dog dare, do you?

Chapter One

A CLIQUE-CLICK IS NOT ONLY THE SOUND A GUN MAKES, BUT IT'S JUST AS DEADLY

WHEN WE FIND OURSELVES IN ANY KIND OF GROUP OR gathering, *cliques* have a way of surfacing. Creeping in before anyone realizes. The word in itself stirs up all sorts of emotions. What about the word *click*? Now there's a word in today's world that can set one's nerves on end. What exactly might we find should we go in search of the definition of a clique or even a click—two words that sound exactly alike, but are spelled differently? Two words that hold completely different meanings—or do they?

Simply put, a *clique* is an exclusive group of people. A *click* is that undeniable sound made when a gun is cocked. So let me get this straight. If you hear the sound *click-click*, either run or hit the deck. Just be sure to cover your head. But what if you hear the sound *clique-clique*? I don't know about you, but I'd probably do the same—run, hit the deck, and cover my head.

Let's focus specifically on *cliques*. Growing up, we all belong to some sort of clique. Whether our particular clique falls into the popular category or not makes very little difference. Unless, of course, we find ourselves at the very bottom rung of the clique ladder. I'd put cliques under the *Evil Things* column. They cause more damage than most realize or even dare to admit. Having come to that conclusion, I must now admit that looking back on elementary, middle, and high school, I definitely belonged to certain cliques. Even as a young adult I belonged to a few cliques. This confession doesn't make them any less evil. It embarrasses me to admit my participation in that which I now condemn. Cliques appear in every part of our lives—school, work, social, and even church. They each carry their own amount of power.

I watched my own children deal with cliques. My oldest daughter was a sucker for cliques, always wanting to be a part of the group. Once, she chose a very destructive group. Her grades fell. We intervened, much to her dismay, at the beginning. Eventually, she came to realize that cliques meant she couldn't be the person she knew herself to be. Fun-loving, silly, always laughing, and, most importantly, honest. When she came to terms with that, her need for the clique shriveled up and died.

Cliques weren't as enticing to my other two daughters, although they were very aware of them. My middle daughter has always been an old soul. Very mature for her age. Although she got bullied once, she also got even. We laugh about it now. She pretty much thumbed her nose at cliques and took some heat for it. My youngest simply ignored them. Or rather, she chose to deal with them tomorrow. We called her our Scarlett O'Hara kid. Sometimes she'd make wistful statements about wanting to belong to a certain clique, only to be met with a tongue lashing from my middle daughter.

Of course, just because a person belongs to a group of friends doesn't necessarily mean that group constitutes a clique. Most groups of friends welcome newcomers. The more the merrier. Cliques specifically define themselves as exclusive groups that don't typically put out a welcome mat. I imagine school cliques typically cause more psychological damage than workplace cliques, because as we age, depending on how we grow into maturity, cliques no longer strangle us. But children in elementary, middle, and high school, find themselves neck-deep in cliques. I submit that children of this age appear ill-equipped to handle the cliques they encounter. They definitely need parental guidance.

My experiences in the workplace, neighborhoods, churches, and Sunday school classes taught me that cliques are most often the norm. Breaking into those cliques without a formal invitation is certainly a feat most fail to accomplish. The majority of cliques seem happy with their closed group of members.

When my husband and I have found ourselves in a new situation—looking for a new church home or organizations to join—the clique factor always plays a huge part in our decision. When I look at volunteering for something, if I see even a hint of a clique, I walk away. My husband, on the other hand, enjoys taunting cliques. He says there's nothing more satisfying than watching them squirm as you ignorantly attempt to stumble your way into their special group. Frankly, I don't possess the patience.

Young people ruin their lives, or even take their lives, all for the sake of a clique. That's precisely why cliques are not only dangerous but deadly.

Who could ever forget the tragedies of Columbine or Virginia Tech? The shooters in each of these terrible events, by all accounts, appeared to those who knew them as loners. Not clique-related? Well, maybe/maybe not. Columbine began when two teenagers killed thirteen people. Then killed themselves. Virginia Tech began when one twenty-three-year-old killed thirty-two people. Then killed himself.

School shootings go all the way back to the 1700s, each one with its own story. From what is known as the Pontiac's Rebellion involving four Lenape Indians in 1764 to shootings in New York City in 1867 all the way up to current times. If cliques played a part in any of them, including Columbine or Virginia Tech, my bet is we will ever know for sure. While looking back over some of these events, I don't recall seeing in writing that cliques caused these people to do these heinous things. But I would imagine events of this type certainly could result from the presence of a clique, simply because they are that dangerous.

Now we must look at that *click* word. Think it dangerous? How about deadly? You bet! I never want to hear that sound anywhere near my person. I have great respect for the word. Growing up, my daddy taught me how to use a gun. But before he taught me how to *use* a gun, he taught me to *respect* a gun. Disrespected guns become deadly.

Certainly in the Bill of Rights, the second amendment to the Constitution, gives people the right to bear arms. Along with that right, one bears a great responsibility. That responsibility is the respect one needs for the arms one bears.

A click can be the difference between life and death. Another thing my daddy taught me about guns—if you ever get to the point where you pull a gun on someone; make sure you are prepared to pull the trigger. I remember the first time he showed me how to use a gun, or should I say rifle. Well, let's just say the thing was bigger than me, and let's just say it had a kick I'll never forget. Along with using a gun, he also taught me to know my rights as a gun owner. It's important.

Once I learned the art of respecting a gun, I never feared it. The person on the other end of the gun, well, that's another story. The click of a gun pointed at any part of your body makes for a most sobering experience. **Click, click!** Could there be any other sound so terrifying? Perhaps, but I'd put that sound at the top of the list. That's precisely why clicks are not only dangerous but deadly.

Should you ever want to see what the Bible says about **cliques**, 1 Corinthians 1:10 might be a good place to start. It reads: "I appeal to you, brothers and sisters, in the name of our Lord Jesus Christ, that all of you agree with one another in what you say and that there be no divisions among you, but that you be perfectly united in mind and thought." How's that for smacking down cliques?

Galatians 6:1-5 pretty much nails it for me. It reads: "Brothers and sisters, if someone is caught in a sin, you who live by the Spirit should restore that person gently. But watch yourselves, or you also may be tempted. Carry each other's burdens, and in this way you will fulfill the law of Christ. If anyone thinks they are something when they are not, they deceive themselves. Each one should test their own actions. Then they can take pride in themselves alone, without comparing themselves to someone else, for each one should carry their own load." So, cliques never work toward the good. They alienate us from one another. They puff us up, making us believe we are more than we really are.

Since cliques have a tendency to entice us, Proverbs 1:10-19 speaks clearly to dealing with such enticements. It tells us they lie in wait not only for the young. Many adults fall under the spell of enticement, leading them to participate in cliques as well.

It surprised me to find several poems written about cliques. The majority of them use words like crying, cruel, whispers, giggles, rumor, jerk, wimp, hurt, pain, and hate. All words with the capability of tearing down anyone's self-esteem.

Take for instance the song "At Seventeen," written by Janice Ian, released in August of 1975. This song speaks to the very definition of cliques. Not only that, but it reveals the impact cliques have on people. It's a powerful song with a powerful message.

It's a good idea to read or listen to the lyrics of this song. I'll wait.

So how many tissues found their way to the floor after reading that? I believe our actions toward others have profound effects. I've often heard people say, "It doesn't bother me what people think of me. I can handle it. They can like me or not like me. They can call me names. I don't care. I don't lose one bit of sleep over it." Total lies. The fact is we *do* care. I said all those things throughout my life, but there's no getting around it—I do care. I eventually came to realize that I can't control what people think or say. I can only control what I think or say or how I react. Although I care how others perceive me, I am who I am. It then comes down to whether others like me or not. After that I just need to step back and let it go.

When we're young, how others see us is a huge deal. We fret, sweat, worry, and pine away the hours all for the sake of a clique. We need to fit in. It matters. We can't handle the things people say to or about us. We *do* care if people like us or not. We *do* lose sleep over what people think of us or what they call us behind our backs. It matters. That's how a clique can trap us, turning us inside out.

What happens to those who never quite fit in? My take? One of two things. They grow into fabulous human beings with the characteristics of giants. Or, the clique wins—then the click wins.

I remember a girl at my high school that never fit in. The majority of the kids made fun of her because of her weight, her unruly hair, her flawed complexion, and her height. She towered over most of the guys. I always felt rather sorry for her. When she showed up at our twenty-year reunion, nobody, I mean *nobody*, recognized her. All the men just stared at her.

Why? She was drop-dead gorgeous! When we all discovered she was the girl who never fit in back in high school, the one all the kids made fun of, well, let us just say, revenge truly can be sweet. The transformation that took place over the years astonished us all.

But the best part? Not only was she beautiful on the outside, her beauty continued on to the inside. I'm sure that inward beauty had always been there. We were just too immature as teens to recognize it. Her graciousness was astonishing. She treated everyone with kindness. Impressive. No, humbling. The clique died that night.

Whether you hear a clique or a click, how you deal with it determines your destiny. Just remember along the way that a clique-click is not only the sound a gun makes, but it's just as deadly!

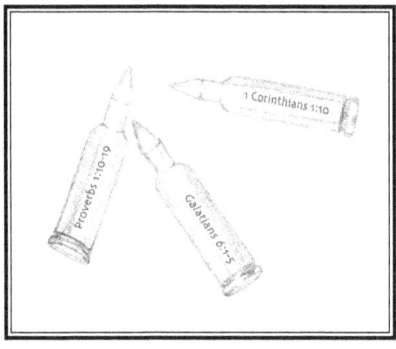

Chapter Two

BEWARE OF THE TROJAN HORSE

What exactly *is* the Trojan War and the story of the Trojan horse? If you're like me, you find history and Greek Mythology amazingly interesting. Remember the movie *Troy*? Two really good-looking guys played the parts of Achilles and Paris. Trojan War! Now, remember the wooden horse in the movie? Trojan horse! Yes!

As I recall from learning about the whole Trojan War/Horse thing in school, it went something like this: The Trojan War started primarily because Paris of Troy kidnapped Helen, a most beautiful woman, from her husband, Menelaus, the king of Sparta, a city in Greece. Of course, this angered Menelaus. He sent a thousand ships to get Helen back. Hence the phrase, "The face that launched a thousand ships."

The Greeks, unfortunately, underestimated the people of Troy. They soon learned just how hard it would be to defeat them. You see, Troy sat inside these tall, strong walls. Consequently, the Greeks found it quite difficult to get inside the city.

According to legend, the war raged on for ten years. In fact, Homer's epic classic *The Iliad* actually starts in the middle of the Trojan War.

Finally, tired of the war and tired of trying to defeat Troy, one of the Greek kings, Odysseus of Ithaca, developed this brilliant plan. They'd build a large wooden horse—large enough to store several Greek soldiers in its belly—then attach it to a set of four wheels and park it outside of the gates of Troy as a peace offering to the Trojans. Then they would pretend to sail away, making it appear as though they'd given up the fight. However, they only sailed around the corner, just out of eyesight of the soldiers standing guard atop Troy's city walls.

To make sure the plan went off without a hitch, they

planted a Greek soldier just outside the gate. When the Trojans found the horse and saw that the Greeks in fact sailed away, the soldier allowed himself to be discovered. He told them his fellow Greeks hated him, that they'd left him behind, and that they left the horse as an offering to Athena, the goddess of wisdom.

Afraid of upsetting Athena, the Trojans rolled the horse right into the city, the Greek soldiers quiet inside its belly. The Trojans were so happy the Greeks sailed away that they threw a huge party to celebrate the end of the war. After everyone partied himself into a drunken stupor, they fell asleep. The Greek soldiers emerged from the belly of the horse and killed all the guards on the walls. By this time, the Greek ships hiding around the corner had sailed back to shore. The soldiers signaled for them to attack. Consequently, all the Trojan men were killed. The women and children were taken back to Greece as slaves.

Now I'm sure there's a moral to this story somewhere. Something like—*beware of the Trojan horse*! Whether or not the Trojan War or the Trojan horse is fact or myth is debated frequently. Nevertheless, I find it all pretty interesting.

So, after all of this, what's really with the warning that is the title of this writing? Simply put, if the Trojan horse story means anything, it means, we should always beware of enemies bearing gifts. Or, more simply put, the old adage, "All that glitters is not gold."

The Trojan horse brought death to the city of Troy. I think that's what happens to most of us who get taken in by things that look too good to be true. Many of us fall into the trap of naiveté, believing something is more than it really is. The Trojans allowed the Greeks to deceive them. Deception is a powerful tool. The Trojan horse was an ingenious plan. Unfortunately for the Trojans, they fell for it.

The Bible speaks to words like deception, entrapment, trickery, defrauding, duping, and outwitting. They all appear in the very first Book of the Bible—Genesis. God barely finished creating everything when in Genesis 3:1–5 we already see the fall of man—not unlike the fall of Troy.

Instead of the Greeks doing the deceiving, it's the serpent—better known as Satan. It reads like this: "Now the serpent was more crafty than any of the wild animals the Lord God had made. He said to the woman, "Did God really say, 'You must not eat from any tree in the garden?'" The woman said to the serpent, "We may eat fruit from the trees in the garden, but God did say, 'You must not eat fruit from the tree that is in the middle of the garden, and you must not touch it, or you will die.'" "You will not certainly die," the serpent said to the woman. "For God knows that when you eat from it your eyes will be opened, and you will be like God, knowing good and evil.""

Even from the beginning of time people have been deceived by those around them. Adam and Eve turned out to be no match for the serpent. His deception went to the heart of their venerability. That which we are forbidden we want all the more. The Greeks went to the heart of the Trojan's vulnerability—their pride. They used that pride to conquer them.

The Bible doesn't stop at Genesis when speaking to deception. Ephesians 5:6–7 tells us not to allow others to deceive us with "empty words." Sometimes first loves are like that.

My first love crushed me to the bone with empty words of devotion. While at a party, I caught him smooching on some other girl. It broke my heart. I was 15. Empty words are little devils in disguise that fool even the most mature of us.

I remembered that first love when my middle daughter

had her heart broken for the first time. We cried buckets together. But we learn, don't we?

In Matthew 7:15–23 Jesus warns us about false prophets who come to us in "sheep's clothing." As in the story of the Trojan horse, we see the results of those who deceive. It ain't pretty. What then happens to those pitiful ones who fall for the deceptions? For the Trojans, physical death. For Adam and Eve, the end of paradise in Eden. Let's not forget the serpent, who was required to crawl on his belly and eat dust for the rest of his life. That's no picnic in my mind.

Sometimes, however, like the Greeks, the deceiver basks in the glory of victory. But for how long? If memory serves, Greece eventually declined and ultimately fell. War, conflict within the communities, loss of trade and military power, clashing of the classes, disloyalty, and laziness were the primary causes of that decline. What once towered above all others as a great nation became a nation of failure. Some may say Greece suffered the consequences of their deceit. I'd agree.

Greece seemed to decline from the inside out. I've heard it said that the way to conquer a nation or people is to do it from the inside out. When a civilization turns on itself, it falls. Is it any wonder, then, that when razing a building the explosives are placed on the inside? The plunger is pushed. The building falls. That's exactly how the Greeks deceived the Trojans. They got inside when they couldn't defeat them from the outside.

When I look around this magnificent country of ours, I get this sick feeling in my belly that we're slowly collapsing from the inside out. I look at the direction in which some circles seem to be traveling. Should we be concerned as a nation? Is there a Trojan horse sitting in every port? Sitting there waiting for the party to begin? Are we being presented with beautiful packages wrapped up in shiny, eye-catching paper, tied ever so neatly with the perfect bow, inside of which, we're told, is a magnificent gift, one that will bring us peace and harmony? A gift that's more glorious than we might ever imagine. A gift that will bring on a feeling of security, pleasure, and calmness. That will make everything better. Plus, it's free. It would be rude to decline. There's no danger associated with such gifts. It's a time for celebration. Right?

We think nothing of the true contents, only that we perceive them to be beautiful on the outside. It's a time for celebration. And, celebrate we do. As did the Trojans.

Parents always want to believe they've left their children with great knowledge. When looking back over the things I've taught my girls, I sincerely hope I taught them to ask questions until they understand, never to put all their eggs in one basket, and never accept things at face value. More importantly, I hope I taught them to beware of Trojan horses.

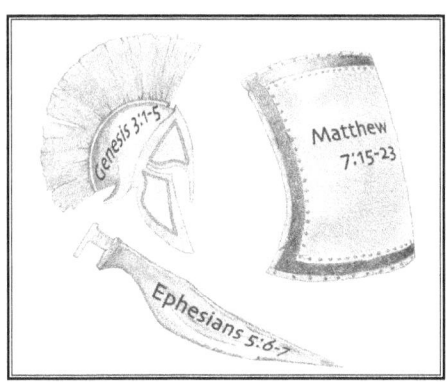

Chapter Three

CORPORATE GENTLEMAN OR CORPORATE CAD?

"The animals are running the zoo." That's what my daddy used to say. After over forty years of working in the corporate world, I've discovered more cads than gentlemen. It's a challenge. I certainly can't be the only one who thinks some corporations have gone mad.

I understand technology, driving in the fast lane, and all the silly things people like to put out there in defense of the so-called new age. What does that term mean anyway? New Age? New in relation to what?

The first time I heard this term I thought, "What is a new age? Is it something different from just being thirty or forty or fifty?" Even now that I actually know its definition, it makes no sense. There's New Age music, New Age religion. The ever-popular New Age movement. On top of that we also must endure many Millennials.

It concerns me that some corporations seem caught up in this new age philosophy, resulting in the creation of unsavory people. Metaphysical types if you will.

Prior generations stayed employed at corporations for their entire working careers. They either climbed up the corporate ladder through hard work and determination, or they were content to be in the job they were in until they retired. Some corporations were run by people with integrity. Not all, mind you. Still, more than in recent years. They wanted the best not only for the corporation but also for the employees who made it run.

The smartest thing a corporate big-shot can do is feed into the morale of his employees. A successful corporate gentleman celebrates the accomplishments of his employees. He incites their morale. He encourages their morals, leading them toward becoming hard-working, responsible, ever-striving members of his team. He puts the needs of them before his own. Why? Because he knows that people who possess a sense of honor plus respect will work their butts off for those to whom they report. They'll go to the mat on their behalf.

Corporate cads do just the opposite.

On my more cynical days, I wonder if there are any corporations left being run by people of substance. If so, where are they? That only leaves us with mom and pop companies that are typically run by honorable people.

Sadly, a corporate cad, unlike a corporate gentleman, will run a company into the ground. Then when the business starts to decline, these guys act surprised. They caused the collapse. They went in directions no sane person would go. They made bad decisions and did not allow anyone to question them. All of a sudden, they can't figure out what's happened to the corporation they were hired to lead. They pretend to possess virtues and/or morals when clearly they don't. They put on a public façade, which places them in the category known as hypocrites.

The Bible speaks clearly about hypocrites. Matthew 6:5-8 tells us: "And when you pray, do not be like the hypocrites, for they love to pray standing in the synagogues and on the street corners to be seen by others. Truly I tell you, they have received their reward in full. But when you pray, go into your room, close the door and pray to your Father, who is unseen. Then your Father, who sees what is done in secret, will reward you. And when you pray, do not keep on babbling like pagans, for they think they will be heard because of their many words. Do not be like them, for your Father knows what you need before you ask him."

Matthew 7:3-5 gives another great instruction regarding

hypocrites. It calls us to look inward at our own flaws before pointing out the flaws of those around us. Matthew calls it looking for the speck in the eye of others when we should be focusing on the log we carry around in our own.

A corporate cad thinks of himself as gold but those in his charge as disposable tin. But here's the rub. Tin is used to coat other metals to prevent corrosion, to protect it from rusting. So while those corporate cads look down on their employees, corporate gentlemen hold them up. It's because they know who and what makes or breaks a corporation. By the way—gold is highly malleable and ductile.

Corporate gentlemen understand the quality of the people they employ. They follow the rule of principle. A corporate gentleman is a successful leader who puts his employees above himself. He enjoys and celebrates the success of those he employs. He brings to the table a guidebook of morals, ethics, consistency, stableness, regularity, and steadiness. He leads with an iron hand, but not one that is so heavy it crushes those beneath it.

The best boss I ever had possessed all the qualities of a corporate gentleman. I busted my behind for him, going far above the calling of the job. He shared the successes and failures of our department with me when clearly not required to do so. He made me feel part of the process. Part of the team. An asset, if you will. Sadly, I never encountered another like him.

All of this brings to mind the following: "When your merchandise went out on the seas, you satisfied many nations; with your great wealth and your wares you enriched the kings of the earth. Now you are shattered by the sea in the depths of the waters; your wares and all your company have gone down with you. All who live in the coastlands are appalled at you; their kings shudder with horror and their faces are distorted with fear. The merchants among the nations scoff at you; you have come to a horrible end and will be no more." Wow! This just might be the best definition of a corporate cad ever. To think, it came from Ezekiel 27:33– 36. I think that's pretty amazing.

I once knew a man of great character. Others who knew him thought the same. They described him with words like honesty and integrity. He worked for a very successful corporation. Exceptionally powerful. This guy spent years developing his industry knowledge. He became well respected in his field. He met and befriended many powerful people. But, as times changed, new leaders emerged. A different philosophy took hold, edging out this good guy.

Over time, the new leadership proved to be inadequate, bringing harsh consequences. The good guy extended a helping hand of friendship to the new leadership only to have it quickly slapped away. The once reputable business shrank to nothing. So, what about my friend? The good guy? Well, he went on to bigger and better things.

Watching this man in this corporation always reminded me of Revelation 18:10: "Terrified at her torment, they will stand far off and cry: 'Woe! Woe to you, great city, you mighty city of Babylon! In one hour your doom has come!'" So became the doom of my friend's company.

The difference between a corporate gentleman and a corporate cad is quite simple. It's how they handle the responsibility of their prosperity. What, exactly, are we looking for when we search out employment, knowing full well this is where we will spend the majority of our waking hours? For those of us who take pride in what we do, this can be daunting. We spend years developing our talents, studying our craft, sharpening our skills—for what? Just to say we've arrived? Competition is fierce. Corruption is fiercer. It all boils down to this. Who do you want to work for? Corporate Gentleman *or* Corporate Cad?

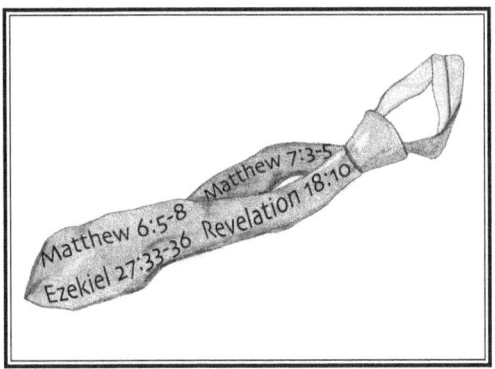

Chapter Four

CRAZY OLD PEOPLE

*G*ROWING OLD. DOES ANYONE DO THAT GRACEFULLY? IF I could wish for anything, I would wish to grow old gracefully. I'm well into my sixties, which means I've passed the halfway point. Old age looms in the not-so-distant future. At the age of twenty-one, I saw sixty as bordering on ancient, with one foot in the grave and one foot on the banana peel, as they say. I certainly couldn't imagine myself pushing sixty, much less seventy. But here I stand with those of us who graduated from high school in 1970 or earlier.

I've recently reconnected with many people I knew from high school. It's been a wonderful experience to talk with them over the waves of the Internet, to share our lives with each other, to talk about how time has treated us these past forty-plus years. Posting pictures of our families, our children, our grandchildren. Sharing milestones with one another. Looking back, I can't help but wonder where the years went. It's amazing to see the faces of the people I called friends as teenagers, faces now lined with the signs of living. Hair streaked with the color that comes from having children or simply the experiences of life.

Funny how crazy old people come into our lives. Funnier still how we relate to them. Listening to body functions that no human should be subjected to, much less tolerate. Keeping a straight face around them seems more of a challenge than one realizes. Smells that make one wonder where in the world these people hang out. Crabby attitudes that make a person want to run themselves off a cliff just to get away. We hope, we pray we won't turn out like the crazy old people we encounter, all the while knowing somewhere in the recesses of our minds that's exactly what will happen. Pretty scary stuff when you think about it.

I remember this crazy old man who lived down the street

from us when our children were little. Every Saturday this guy went out and dug a trench all around the perimeter of his yard. We could never figure out why he did this. We even thought of stopping by one Saturday while he was out digging just to ask. Common sense prevailed. Maybe not a great idea. He probably would have smacked us down with his shovel. We eventually came to the realization that he was a crazy old man.

There have been millions of jokes written about crazy old people. Some are funny but most are quite unflattering. The really crude ones that I'm sure I laughed hardily at as a younger person don't seem so funny to me now. However, as I *gracefully* age, I've found that my friends seem to be sending me way too many jokes about old people. Not funny.

George Burns was once quoted as saying, "You know you're getting old when you stoop to tie your shoelaces and wonder what else you could do while you're down there." I love it! Truman Capote who was quoted as saying, "Life is a moderately good play with a badly written third act." Finally, G.K. Chesterton reportedly said, "Don't ever take a fence down until you know the reason it was put up." That's pretty good advice. We all tend to tear things down before we know the reasons they were put there in the first place.

One might wonder how that last quote fits in with the old age topic and crazy old people. Anyone who is over the age of fifty will attest to the fact that one should never walk into a room and move something, because you probably put it there for a reason. You just can't remember the reason. Then there's this: one should never salt their food before tasting it, because you probably already salted it and just don't remember doing it. Tearing down a fence is the same thing. The consequences might not be so good.

In the end, no pun intended, Edward W. Howe is quoted as saying it best, "If you don't learn to laugh at troubles, you won't have anything to laugh at when you grow old." How true is that? All the things I laugh at now were traumatic in my younger days. If we can't laugh at the craziness of life, old age will most definitely win. I absolutely don't intend to allow old age to win.

I once knew a sweet elderly lady who smiled all the time. I often wondered how, with all her ailments, she remained joyful. She told me that life is more than just aches and pains. If you focus on the pain, you miss the living. This amazing lady, who stole our hearts, lived her life as we all should aspire to live ours—a grand old lady. Personally, I think she smiled all the time because she knew something the young don't know—*you're gonna be where I am someday, you young whippersnapper!*

The Bible is filled with verses that speak to growing old or to the elderly. The book of Proverbs is a favorite of mine. Its verses always seem to give me comfort. As it pertains to growing old, Proverbs 16:31 reads: "Gray hair is a crown of splendor; it is attained in the way of righteousness." I don't know about anyone else, but I certainly needed that!

We women often find it difficult to deal with that gray/white hair thing. In men, it's called distinguished. In women, it's called haggard. So when I start stressing over the ever-growing number of gray hairs I find on a daily basis, I remember Proverbs. I remember that our grandchildren are our pride. I couldn't agree with that part more.

The book of Isaiah assures us in chapter 46 verse 4 that God will sustain us in our old age, gray hairs and all. Leviticus 19:32 makes sure we understand in no uncertain terms how to treat the elderly. They should be respected, even to the point of standing in their presence.

Over the years I've developed a new-found respect for the elderly as I watched my mother age, then pass, visited with two amazing women at a nearby assisted living home, seen the passing of those I love due to nothing more than their bodies giving out from a lifetime of living. I would imagine it difficult, at best, to show grace when every part of your body screams old and tired. Those who suffer from the pains or humiliation of old age, and do it with grace, should be admired. Those who don't should be forgiven. We all have limits to which we can bear certain things. Growing old is that kick in the gut that reminds us we're not in control of anything. No matter how hard we try to turn back the clock through all sorts of reconstructive surgeries or even living vicariously through our children, time keeps moving forward. I know I've become more aware of my own mortality over the years.

The wrinkles, the sagging skin continue to disfigure our appearance until we think we just might go mad. We cling to everything new or improved. Whether we dress like those twenty to thirty years younger or hit on those who are twenty to thirty years younger, our compulsive need to stay young will truly be our demise.

The Curious Case of Benjamin Button, a 2008 film whereby the main character ages in reverse, is a prime example of our dream to stay young, to avoid the indignation of growing old. But grow old we must, as it is life's most natural progression.

As we age, all the while watching our children do the same, we should learn to keep Biblical words close to our hearts. Ecclesiastes 12:1–7 reads: "Remember your Creator in the days of your youth, before the days of trouble come and the years approach when you will say, "I find no pleasure in them"—before the sun and the light and the moon and the stars grow dark, and the clouds return after the rain; when the keepers of the house tremble, and the strong men stoop, when the grinders cease because they are few, and those looking through the windows grow dim; when the doors to the street are closed and the sound of grinding fades; when people rise up at the sound of birds, but all their songs grow faint; when people are afraid of heights and of dangers in the streets; when the almond tree blossoms and the grasshopper drags itself along and desire no longer is stirred. Then people go to their eternal home and mourners go about the streets. Remember him—before the silver cord is severed, and the golden bowl is broken; before the pitcher is shattered at the spring, and the wheel broken at the well, and the dust returns to the ground it came from, and the spirit returns to God who gave it."

There will come a time when things get blurry, when our memory dims, when we spill more food on our clothes than we get in our mouth, when we feel the embarrassment of wet pants, or when bodily functions find their way out at the most inopportune times. Yes, that time will indeed come to us all. Before too long, we too, will be one of those crazy old people.

Chapter Five

DOC BAKER NEVER ASKED FOR MONEY UP FRONT

REGINA STONE MATTHEWS

*M*Y HUSBAND AND I ENGAGE IN SOME VERY HEATED discussions regarding healthcare, hospitals, doctors, and doctors' offices. All terrible from where I stand. From inadequate business practices to the overwhelming incompetence, I find myself in that dark place when dealing with the medical industry.

The loudest laugh that ever came out of my face happened when I called my doctor's office to schedule an appointment for my yearly check-up. Naturally, I called to speak to the *scheduler*. Only I don't actually get to speak with the *scheduler* at this juncture. One never actually gets a human being when first calling these places. So I get a recording. It goes something like this:

"Thank you for calling XYZ Doctor's Office (the names have changed to protect the innocent). To hear this message in English press one, in Espanola press two."

I'm in the United States, right? So I press one.

The message continues. "To reach the scheduling department for Dr. Whatever, press one; to reach the scheduling department for Dr. Whenever, press two; to reach the scheduling department for Dr. Whoever press three." It goes on and on and on until finally I hear my doctor's name.

I press *twenty-four*.

The recording keeps going. "You have reached the scheduling department for Dr. (My Doctor), please leave your name, phone number, home address, date of birth, insurance information, social security number, blood type, credit card number (that's just in case they can't get in touch with you when they call you back, that way they can hit your card with a charge for their time), and a brief message. One of our (**wait for it**) *friendly* and *knowledgeable* staff will call you back as soon as possible."

I literally fell on the floor laughing. First of all, it is not always a prerequisite to be *friendly* or *knowledgeable* to get an administrative job at a doctor's office or hospital. The only thing an individual must possess is a killer instinct.

I've read numerous publications regarding doctors who ask for money up front. Not simply co-pay but full amounts. This came as no surprise to me because for the last few years I've been battling with my doctors' offices over this very thing. The main reason is because the people in these doctors' offices don't have a clue as to what they are doing. How do I know this? From personal experience. Way too many times I've been asked for money based on an estimate—which I'm told they got from the insurance company—as to what the insurance is going to pay. So they want the balance which, nine times out of ten, is wrong.

After I pay, they file with the insurance company; the insurance company pays them. I get a copy of the EOB (explanation of benefits) which tells me how much the insurance company actually paid. Now I have to call these *friendly* and *knowledgeable* people to tell them I want my money back. So, I have simply refused to pay up front.

Yep, they hate my guts.

As co-pays and deductibles continue to climb, the patient must come up with this money on the spot. There's always a good and bad side to any issue or procedure. The upside is that patients know right away how much they're going to owe. The downside is that patients are often forced to pay up front or they won't get medical treatment at all.

Too many times I've heard office staff use intimidation tactics in order to get money from the patient. If doctors or hospitals are the ones implementing aggressive tactics, then shame on all of them. Being sick is stressful enough without being bullied. The best rule of thumb is to ask the question regarding payment in advance before visiting the doctor, if at all possible.

At one time, people became doctors for the healing of the sick. Not so much for the money. I remember when doctors really cared. They actually took time to treat a patient. When my mother was a little girl, doctors came to the house. The patient was the priority. The fee was secondary. Not so now. Given the state of healthcare, this might be why we're in our current predicament. Healthcare has long been out of control, with doctors and hospitals spending more time chasing the dollar than caring for the patient. Healthcare is compounded when the government attempts to run it. When that happens we turn over our rights to our own healthcare. It makes for a bumpy ride.

Although it sounds as if I believe there's no such thing as a caring doctor, I actually do believe they are out there—somewhere. They consider it an honor to care for the sick. Yet I know that those types of doctors are few.

Here's a challenge: walk into a hospital or a doctor's office. Ask to see the doctor. What's the first question asked?

Here's another challenge: call the doctor's office. Ask to speak to the doctor. What's the first question asked?

I understand busy. I understand there are nuts out there who try to take advantage. I understand procedure. I also understand a person has to make a living. I don't begrudge anyone making money for their expertise. What I don't understand is unfriendly or incompetent.

There are many medical horror stories out there. When most people go to see the doctor they're in the waiting room a long time past the actual appointment. Could it be that the staff has double-booked the patients? Then the patient sits an extended length of time in the exam room waiting for the doctor to show up. By the time the doctor *does* show up, the examination lasts about two minutes. Hardly enough time to diagnose anything.

Some might say all of this is unfair. Doctors, hospitals, and their staffs are under a great deal of pressure. I don't disagree. Who out there isn't under a great deal of pressure? If people are going to go to all the expense and the endless hours of study to become doctors, they should know what they're getting into before they jump. If you aren't in it for the patients, don't get into it at all.

It's interesting to note that there are countless websites that speak to things like patient advocacy, the empowerment of patients, wrong diagnosis, and questions to ask the doctor. As a patient, you can only hope you are under the care of a doctor who puts you first. Otherwise, it's a rather helpless feeling.

Doctors have been around since prehistoric times. We've gone through several eras. The ancient Egyptian doctors, the Greek doctors, the Roman doctors, the Medieval doctors, the Renaissance doctors, the doctors of the nineteenth century, all the way to now—the doctors of the twenty-first century.

That's a lot of history and learning. Doctors have come a long way since the Stone Age. But the goal is still the same—the healing of the patient.

The Word tells us in Micah 6:6-8: "With what shall I come before the Lord and bow down before the exalted God? Shall I come before him with burnt offerings, with calves a year old? Will the Lord be pleased with thousands of rams, with ten thousand rivers of olive oil? Shall I offer my first born for my transgression, the fruit of my body for the sin of my soul? He has shown you, O mortal, what is good. And what does the Lord require of you? To act justly and to love mercy and to walk humbly with your God." Just might be trying to tell us something about how we treat one another. Be it doctor-to-patient or human-to-human.

The movie *The Doctor* is a great example of the doctor versus the patient. The main character is Dr. Jack MacKee. The tagline on the movie website reads: "He was a doctor who thought he knew it all…until he became a patient." That one line says it all. The movie is based on the true story of a brilliant although arrogant doctor who comes face to face with the realities of being a patient. The funny thing is, he doesn't much like it. You'll have to watch the movie to see how it ends.

If looking at the art of healing, a doctor must first realize that diagnosing diseases or working to beat the disease is all fine. But being a doctor is more than that. It's wanting to be a part of the "art of healing." It's about being human, and understanding that the patient is human too. It's about the healing *for* the patient. Not the money *from* the patient.

Doc Baker was a good doctor and a good man. Remember him? The small-town doctor from Walnut Grove on *Little House on the Prairie*. Doctors in the 1800s were rarely home. They traveled from farm to farm, keeping in touch with their patients, going to them in the middle of the night, in all kinds of weather, in order to deliver babies or care for the sick. Getting paid with chickens, canned goods, a handshake or a hug backed by the promise that the next crop would bring some money and the doc would be at the top of the list of those paid.

Doc Baker never asked for anything. He was about the healing, not the money. He was about the people. Good thing Doc Baker isn't here to see how it all turned out. Although a fictitious character, I'm confident there used to be a lot of Doc Bakers.

The best doctor I ever had defined the title *physician*. He delivered my first child. I was only 19 at the time. Not clue one as to how to be a mother. I sat looking to this man for guidance. Asking question after question after question. Most would have simply dismissed me. This doctor sat with me, answered every question until I ran out of questions. The caring with which he presented himself has stayed with me to this day.

What a pity that today we look at the practice of medicine as a business. When I go to the doctor, it's either as a preventive action or because I'm extremely sick. I want to know that the man or woman I bare my everything to looks at me as a vulnerable human being. That they are there to help make me better. Doctors are a vital part of our lives. We literally put our physical existence in their hands.

When we walk into that office, the only thing we need to think about is getting better. Doc Baker saw to it that his patients knew he cared, knew he would be there for them. He wanted them to know he would do whatever he could to make them better. He was their friend as well as their doctor. By the way, Doc Baker never asked for money up front.

Chapter Six

FINDING YOUR EMOTIONAL INTELLIGENCE

A PLACE CALLED *Common Sense*

Finding your emotional intelligence? What does that mean? It sounds like an oxymoron to me. How do intelligence and emotion even work together? Most of us who find ourselves in an emotional situation seldom, if ever, use intelligence as a basis for our decisions. I've found when I make emotional decisions I always end up regretting them.

Emotional intelligence is not only an awareness of our emotions, but also the ability to manage them. Sounds simple enough, right? So I started thinking about how some people possess the ability to control their emotions while others run completely on emotion.

For me, it depends on the situation. If it involves my family—forget about it. I'm totally emotion-driven. If it involves business or people I have no vested interest in—emotion never enters into the equation. Simply put, I can be ruthless. Maybe not something a person should be proud of, but typically those who can leave the emotion out of their decision making don't regret their decisions.

Then I thought, what about self-control, will power, or impulse control? Seems to me if a person has this emotional intelligence thing going on then these three factors are a piece of cake. Pardon the pun. We also know how these characteristics come into play when it comes to diet! The hardest thing to do is to control our urges when dieting. It goes along with the wanting what we can't have dilemma. So finding one's emotional intelligence falls under the category of being able to control oneself. Makes sense that it might take a good bit of intelligence to accomplish that.

We see people every day, whether out in our world or in TV land, not exercising their emotional intelligence at all.

Sometimes, it's quite funny. Other times, it's quite tragic. No matter what the circumstances, those three types of controls seem pretty important in determining one's character. People who possess an abundance of emotional intelligence find it difficult to deal with people who run on nothing more than instant gratification. These poor schmucks find it difficult to sit still long enough to develop any kind of emotional intelligence. They're looking to satisfy their immediate itch. So where does that leave us? Are we human beings who all house within us this character trait called emotional intelligence? Or are we human beings who all house within us this character trait called instant gratification. Guess it depends on who's making the call.

Hyperbolic discounting is one of those terms that I guarantee will make your head explode if you attempt to search out its meaning. Deferred gratification or delayed gratification is a whole lot easier on the brain. However, if intellectual brains run in the family, then hyperbolic discounting might be worth the research. In my simple world, the only thing that resonates with me is that animals don't work from the emotional intelligence or deferred/delayed gratification standpoint. They work strictly from the hyperbolic discounting standpoint.

Take, for example a bird just sitting around minding its own business. Now, completely invade this bird's personal space and put two buttons in front of it. One button, when pushed, gives the bird food instantly; however, there's a delay on the other button. The bird will try both buttons then settle on the button that gives the food instantly. Animals go for the instant gratification. I know this first hand because there's a dog in our family who loves that instant gratification thing. This dog's motto is *"never* wait!" Go for the food immediately!

Animals simply don't possess the ability to defer or delay their gratification.

Humans, on the other hand, possess the ability to use emotional intelligence, i.e., self-control, will power, or impulse control. But they also possess the ability to lean toward the hyperbolic discounting and/or instant gratification direction.

Here's the buzz about this hyperbolic discounting thing in humans. Test: if individuals are told they can have $100.00 today or $200.00 in a year most will choose the $100.00 today. But if those same individuals are offered $100.00 in five years or $200.00 in six years almost all of them will choose the $200.00 in six years. Is that logical or illogical? That's why hyperbolic discounting is so complex. Figuring out why people are willing to wait that extra year in order to receive more is quite interesting.

I'd never heard of the "Marshmallow Experiment" until I saw the video one Sunday in church. We all laughed so hard our sides hurt. This film represented temptation at its best, and I submit that hyperbolic discounting is simply that—intense temptation.

Let me sum up the essence of the "Marshmallow Experiment." The video opens with the scene of a room with a table and a chair. A teacher brings a kid into the room. Then she sits the kid down at the table. She puts one marshmallow on a plate. Next she tells the kid that the marshmallow is for him. Then she tells him he can either wait, and she will give him another one when she returns, or he can eat it now. She reiterates that if he waits until she returns she'll give him another one making two marshmallows he can eat. Then she leaves the room.

It's fascinating how each of these kids, boys and girls alike, handle this very complex situation. I use the word "complex" because this experiment tests the very core of one's character. Why character? Because from the time the teacher leaves until the time she returns, these kids must decide if they possess emotional intelligence or if they've fallen victim to instant gratification. I couldn't believe how much self-control, will power, and impulse control the majority of these kids exhibited. Plus, it was hilarious to watch how each one of them handled the urge to throw caution to the wind and eat the marshmallow. Only a couple of them said, "Who cares!" and simply ate the marshmallow the moment the teacher left the room.

What impressed me the most with the kids who chose to wait was that she never told them they couldn't eat the marshmallow. In fact she told them they could. She also told them if they didn't eat the marshmallow, they would get another one, which meant, if they waited, they would have more to eat later. That's emotional intelligence—the ability to discern and understand that waiting and saving can actually produce more later on down the road.

I've heard some say that if a person possesses what is classified as good impulse control, this control is often considered a personality trait. That control leads to emotional intelligence. The kids who exercised deferred or delayed gratification were most likely academically successful. Their ability to defer or delay their gratification indicated they understood they would end up with more marshmallows if they waited for the teacher to return. Temptation got the better of a few. Ultimately they received less.

Our ability to wait in life is challenged at every turn. We don't do it well. As I watched the video of the "Marshmallow Experiment," the part that caught my eye was the actual temptation, mainly because our youth struggle with temptation daily. Their lack of experience or maturity makes it difficult for them to resist. Certainly, adults battle with temptation, but those adults who have difficulty with temptation also suffer from immaturity. How many of us have dealt with an immature adult in our past or present? I think it's worse than dealing with an immature teen.

As we grow, our goal is to mature in the various aspects of our life. We mature in our personal and romantic relationships. We mature in our business relationships. More importantly, we mature in our faith. All of this growth takes time. Just like in the "Marshmallow Experiment," time is the key. Waiting, as in the passage of time, grows to patience— my biggest hurdle in life. Those who know me well know patience is definitely not one of my greatest virtues. At times I succeed, but more times than not, I fall miserably short. I look forward to correcting that flaw as I mature! Certainly a few of the kids in the "Marshmallow Experiment" video could teach me a thing or two about the virtue of patience. I should look them up sometime.

As to those who allowed temptation to overrule their emotional intelligence, well, they ended up with no profits at the end of the experiment. They never experienced the pleasure of savoring their accomplishment. Turning a profit eluded them because they gobbled up any profit they might have earned. The thing about instant gratification is that it's gone in an instant, right along with the gratification. Savoring the moment makes the memory of the moment that much sweeter. Maturity helps us realize that fact.

What about this temptation thing? Its definition is strong. It leans toward enticement or allurement. The kids in the

"Marshmallow Experiment" were tempted beyond belief. Not only were they asked to wait, they were asked to look temptation right in the eye. The marshmallow was strategically placed in front of their faces with all its loveliness of shape and smell. Sitting right in front of them was the very thing they were asked to leave alone. The reward? More of what they wanted. The cost? Resisting the urge to indulge before the time elapsed.

We've all been tempted at some point in our life. Even Jesus was tempted. Matthew 4:1-11 tells us: "Then Jesus was led by the Spirit into the wilderness to be tempted by the devil. After fasting forty days and forty nights, he was hungry. The tempter came to him and said, 'If you are the Son of God, tell these stones to become bread.' Jesus answered, 'It is written: 'Man shall not live on bread alone, but on every word that comes from the mouth of God.' Then the devil took him to the holy city and had him stand on the highest point of the temple. 'If you are the Son of God,' he said, 'throw yourself down. For it is written: 'He will command his angels concerning you, and they will lift you up in their hands, so that you will not strike your foot against a stone.' Jesus answered him, 'It is also written: 'Do not put the Lord your God to the test.' Again, the devil took him to a very high mountain and showed him all the kingdoms of the world and their splendor. 'All this I will give you,' he said, 'if you will bow down and worship me.' Jesus said to him, 'Away from me, Satan! For it is written: 'Worship the Lord your God, and serve him only.' Then the devil left him, and angels came and attended him." Nice to know that we're not the only ones tempted by our surroundings or by others. The key is to follow Jesus' example and resist. If we do, we'll profit all the more for it.

It never ceases to amaze me how much we learn from one another. Especially how much we can learn from kids. In the "Marshmallow Experiment" video these children portrayed every emotion of trying to overcome temptation. Here's a list of a few of the tactics they used to keep from actually eating the marshmallow:

1. Staring it down.
2. Smelling it.
3. Trying not to look at it.
4. Closing their eyes and touching it.
5. Rubbing it across their lips.
6. Licking their fingers and touching it then putting their fingers in their mouths.
7. Picking it up quickly and then putting it back down on the plate.
8. Closing their eyes so they couldn't see it.
9. Pounding their head on the table.
10. Pretending to put it in their mouth.
11. Kissing it.
12. Nibbling it, but just a little.

Priceless! A couple of the kids stood out for me. They were determined not to eat that marshmallow. I believe they would have sat there and never eaten it, no matter how long the teacher stayed away. Incidentally, she was gone only twenty minutes which seemed, I am sure, like an eternity to these kids.

I'm reminded of a verse in the Book of 1 Corinthians 10:13 that reads: "No temptation has overtaken you except what is common to mankind. And God is faithful; he will not let you be tempted beyond what you can bear. But when you are tempted, he will also provide a way out so that you can endure it." I guess that's where the pounding of the head on the table comes into play.

I couldn't have been more proud of those who made it through the experiment, winning out over the temptation. For those whose instant gratification overcame their emotional intelligence, well, better luck next time. Mark 14:38 pertains to them as it reads: "Watch and pray so that you will not fall into temptation. The spirit is willing, but the flesh is weak."

Let's face it, maturing is difficult at best. We must do things like use good manners, exude confidence in ourselves, keep our temper in check, exhibit grace when being complimented or criticized, be helpful, don't curse, speak properly, and always try to have a good attitude. Sounds like all the things we learned in elementary school. I guess some of us got it and some of us didn't. Nevertheless, all of these things when learned and utilized lead to maturity.

I've watched my daughters grow into their own maturity. They still act silly when they get together, giggling and poking fun at one another. But I sit back proudly watching them in their daily lives. One is a mother of three and business owner, one a devoted businesswoman, and one a mother and second-grade school teacher. To think, they all belong to me. Well maybe my husband had a little bit to do with it. Please don't tell him that because he gets cocky when he thinks he's contributed to something grand. He tends to leave his emotional intelligence at the door.

Maturing into the person we all need and want to be should be our ultimate goal. To be the person God intended us to be, we must overcome temptation when all we want to do is give in. If nothing else, we should all be motivated toward being examples to our kids. Maybe even being examples to any kid we come in contact with. So whenever the need to eat the marshmallow creeps in, take a moment. Remember the payoff for waiting. Remember that instant gratification ends in an instant. Remember words like self-control, will power, impulse control, deferred, delayed, and instant gratification. And that ever-popular hyperbolic discounting. Make a note to not get caught with your maturity level on empty.

By the way, good luck in finding your emotional intelligence.

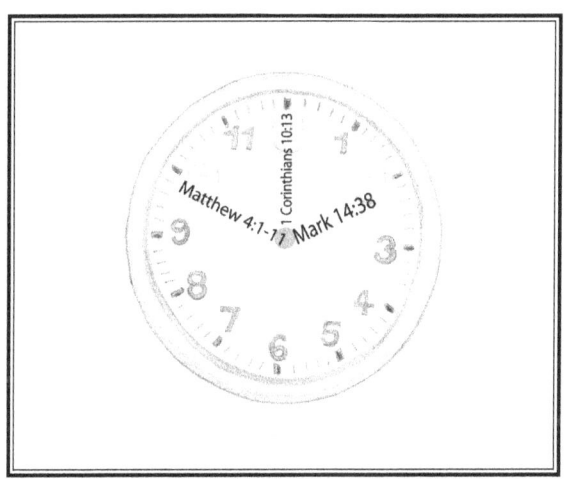

Chapter Seven

HANGING ON TO BAD MESSAGES

A PLACE CALLED *Common Sense*

WHEN WE HANG ON TO BAD THINGS, WE PUT OURSELVES in a stagnant position. Hanging on to bad messages works much in the same way. Remember the movie *Invincible*? What a great movie about perseverance, determination, and heart. It's based on the life of thirty-year-old Vince Papale who ended up playing football for the Philadelphia Eagles. Papale, a bartender from South Philly, decided at the urging of his friends, to try out for the Eagles. Newly appointed head coach Dick Vermeil had decided to hold open tryouts. Of course, this didn't sit well with anyone in the league, much less the fans. Against all odds, Vince Papale not only tried out but actually made the team.

Although his confidence level came in at zero, he had talent. He took that talent, sucked it up, and tried out, all the while never really believing in the possibility of making the team. Sadly, one bad message almost did him in because he believed it. That's what happens when we hang on to bad messages. The coach believed in Vince more than Vince believed in himself. When Vince made the team, he finally tore up the message. The rest, as they say, is history.

How many of us are like that? Why do we hang on to bad messages anyway? They certainly don't build up our self-esteem—or do they? Some might argue that bad messages fuel determination. Like telling someone they can't do something or can't have something. That can make certain people want it that much more. They tend to go out of their way or do whatever it takes in order to obtain the thing that's forbidden to them. So I guess we could say bad messages can cause a double effect. I lean more toward bad messages holding us back. But whether or not bad messages make us determined or insecure, sometimes even our determination can lead us in the wrong direction.

Bad messages, when played over and over inside our heads, eventually convince us we have nothing to offer. We get this weariness about us that announces to others we feel we're less than they are.

People aren't the only carriers of bad messages. Look at the bad messages that come to us by way of TV, movies, and music. The media seems to take pride in spewing out bad messages. Messages we shouldn't lend an ear to but find ourselves mesmerized by. It's a sickness. At some point, we can no longer distinguish between the good and the bad message. We get so caught up in the drama we allow the bad message to bypass our brain and make their way to our hearts. In the innermost part of our hearts the seed is planted. The bad message is left to root, growing until it strangles our very spirit. That's the victory of the bad message—the killing of the spirit.

As we raise our children, we try to instill in them the importance of a positive attitude. We want them to seek out good messages. Throughout their growing up years, we encourage them to always put forth their best effort and to strive for excellence. To surround themselves with those who share their same values. When they encounter people who attempt to tear them down, we pray we've taught them the power of being a good example. We can't always shield our children from bad messages, but we can equip them to handle them. Our children are faced with bad messages every single day of their lives, just as were we when we were kids. The difference is the bad messages from way back in the olden times were inflicted on us face to face. Today bad messages take flight. They crawl through the wires of the Internet and, like a contagious disease, they go airborne with no possibility of locating the host in an effort to stifle the infection. These bad messages can devastate the recipient.

As a youngster, I faced a boatload of bad messages delivered by other kids. It hurt to the core. I found myself being cornered in the hall at school while three or four boys threw spitballs at me while the girls laughed. Not my idea of a good message moment. I cried a lot during my elementary school years, until I met a girl named Lois and a boy named Sandy. They convinced me to tell my parents about the bullies. I didn't want to at first, but when I did, it turned out to be the best decision. My daddy taught me how to stand up to the bad messages. He taught me how to defend myself. Ultimately, with the help of my newly found friends, I put my daddy's good message into action and came out the victor.

How are bad messages created then delivered? They initially start with the tongue. From there, they can be handwritten, texted, or thrown out onto social media. Remember the old saying, "Once on the lips, forever on the hips?" This can be applied to bad messages as well. Once the bad message is spun, forever it will run. They can literally crush us.

How often do we hear news reports about young people killing themselves over bad messages published on the Internet? It all starts with the lashing out of the tongue. The Bible speaks quite clearly to the managing of our tongue. Matthew 12:36–37 reads: "But I tell you that everyone will have to give account on the day of judgment for every empty word they have spoken. For by your words you will be acquitted, and by your words you will be condemned." Likewise, Psalm 34:13 reads: "keep your tongue from evil and your lips from telling lies." There's no mistaking the meaning of these verses.

Our tongue is the most destructive part of our body. The

bad messages we deliver with our tongue can do more damage than we can imagine. "Sticks and stones may break my bones, but words can never harm me," is a saying with a lost meaning. During my childhood, parents used to recite that to their children when some hateful kid at school said bad things to them or about them. It was a noble effort to take away the sting of the words, but it never really helped. Words *do* hurt. The tongue is like a sword. It can cut right down to a person's soul. I submit that God would rather we speak words of comfort. Words of encouragement.

Still, I've never advocated backing away from an attack. Defending ourselves is altogether different. It falls into the category of standing up for something. The key is to find the best way to control our tongues in order to open up our hearts. It certainly isn't an easy task. Emotions get the better of us. Sometimes, evil creeps in. It takes over. Sometimes, people are just plain spiteful. Psalm 19:14 gives us a great instruction on controlling our words. It reads: "May these words of my mouth and this meditation of my heart be pleasing in your sight, Lord, my Rock and my Redeemer."

Finally, the Book of James speaks to how our tongue can really get us into trouble. James 3:3–6 reads: "When we put bits into the mouths of horses to make them obey us, we can turn the whole animal. Or take ships as an example. Although they are so large and are driven by strong winds, they are steered by a very small rudder wherever the pilot wants to go. Likewise, the tongue is a small part of the body, but it makes great boasts. Consider what a great forest is set on fire by a small spark. The tongue also is a fire, a world of evil among the parts of the body. It corrupts the whole body, sets the whole course of one's life on fire, and is itself set on fire by hell." Very necessary words to show us how the tongue can deliver bad messages that can hurt.

Physical abuse scars the body, but the tongue can scar the human spirit. One word or sentence can scar a person for life, taking years to repair. Breaking the spirit can shut down a person. Yet although the human spirit is a very delicate thing, it's also very powerful.

John F. Kennedy was quoted as saying, *"I am certain that after the dust of centuries has passed over our cities, we, too, will be remembered not for victories or defeats in battle or in politics, but for our contribution to the human spirit."* I agree. It motivates us to succeed. It's the driving force that wins the battle. Contributing to the human spirit is essential. Hanging on to bad messages is extrinsic. I once read that physical strength is measured by what we can carry; if that is true, then spiritual strength is measured by what we can bear. Good words.

We're told by doctors to always talk to people in comas. Certainly we don't send bad messages. We send good messages. We sit with loved ones who are in comas, sick, or drifting in and out of consciousness, and we talk about the good stuff. Those positive messages lift the spirit giving the person a reason to live. I've known surgeons who talk to their patients as they're going under anesthesia. They tell them the operation will be a success, that they will feel better. They offer up good messages because the subconscious hears the words and reacts.

To embrace the good messages, all it takes is tearing up the bad messages and throwing them away. Too simple? It's probably the most difficult thing a person being tormented by bad messages, can do. It really does take courage, but as the Wizard of Oz said to the Cowardly Lion, *"As for you, my fine friend, you're a victim of disorganized thinking."* The Wizard wants the Cowardly

Lion to understand that all he needs is a medal. It represents that good message the Cowardly Lion needed. The Wizard of Oz hangs the "Triple Cross" around the neck of the Cowardly Lion. Miraculously, he is cowardly no more. A positive message won out over a bad message. The bad message the Cowardly Lion carried with him his entire life was torn up and thrown away.

Words like faith, hope, and love all send out messages of a brighter future. Good messages, not bad ones. Positive messages, not negative. Uplifting messaged, not depressing. That should be our goal.

Vince Papale finally got the message. Tear it up! From that point forward, he no longer fell into the category the bad message tried to put him in because he chose to walk away from it. There are those who never get away from the bad messages. They carry them throughout their lives. They live each day replaying those destructive tunes in their heads until everyone around them believes it—including them. It need not be that way. If faith, hope, and love aren't a part of our vocabulary then we need to look them up, learn them. Let them be the tune we play over and over in our minds. Let us not be among the ones hanging on to bad messages.

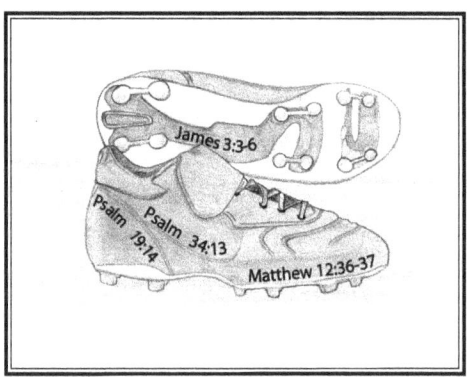

Chapter Eight

I'VE SEEN HELL AND I DON'T WANT TO GO THERE!

"Where exactly is hell?" you ask. Here's the answer. Any local supercenter on a Saturday. Better yet, on the Saturday before the Super Bowl! I see those heads nodding, Yes! Yes! Yes! I'll do anything to keep from going to one of those places on a Saturday. Sometimes it can't be avoided, and so I've come to believe that supercenters on a weekend are a way for us to catch a glimpse of hell. We know for certain that we never want to go there. In their defense, the local supercenter isn't the only hell. There are lots of them out there.

We know that hell is that place of torment and misery where the wicked go when they die. It's always sounded pretty scary to me. The Bible's definition is definitely scary. The Book of 2 Thessalonians 1:8–9 tells us: "He will punish those who do not know God and do not obey the gospel of our Lord Jesus. They will be punished with everlasting destruction and shut out from the presence of the Lord and from the glory of his might." For me that's the most powerful definition of hell—the separation from God. I've always believed true hell would be just that.

How one lives without God is something I truly don't understand. The Book of Revelation has always been somewhat of a mystery to me. It's a difficult book to comprehend. However, some passages speak directly to the reader without confusion. Such is Revelation 20:13, which tells us we will be judged for the things we've done. Additionally, Revelation 21:8 warns us that if we are cowards, unbelievers, vile, murders or sexually immoral we will face exceptional punishment. It doesn't overlook those who are in the practice of black magic or are idolaters or liars. This punishment is considered the second death.

Finally, Revelation 6:8 tells us: "I looked, and there before me was a pale horse! Its rider was named Death, and Hades was following close behind him. They were given power over a fourth of the earth to kill by sword, famine and plague, and by the wild beasts of the earth." Clearly, Revelation doesn't mess around with the definition of hell.

I've always loved Rod Serling. Could they have picked anyone better to host *Twilight Zone* and *Night Gallery*? Those who know anything about him know him as an excellent screenwriter and novelist. You can also add American military hero to his resume. Along with being awarded the Purple Heart and Bronze Star after serving in World War II from 1943 until 1945, he also boxed while serving in the military and didn't do too shabby at that, either.

From what I understand, Mr. Serling suffered from nightmares, which inspired many of his writings. *Twilight Zone* lasted five seasons. In 1969, *Night Gallery* aired. I can vividly remember an episode of *Night Gallery* entitled "Hell's Bells." This episode aired on November 17, 1971. It starred John Astin, Jody Gilbert, Hank Worden, John J. Fox, and Ceil Cabot. Astin, being the main character, not only saw hell; he literally went there.

John Astin plays the part of this stoned-out-of-his-mind hippie. While under the influence one night, he crashes his car and dies. This guy fully expects he's going to hell. In fact, he's prepared himself for it. Or so he thinks. Upon arriving in hell, he finds himself in a waiting room. Not what he expected, but he can wait. His vision of hell includes being with the so-called *prince of darkness* along with all the other tormented souls and dancing demons. Suddenly, a fire door opens. Now this is more like it, he's thinking, as he walks through what he believes are the absolute jaws of hell. But he finds himself in yet another sitting room. This place isn't his idea of hell, either. But there's hope, because he spots a jukebox in the corner of the room. Excited now, he pushes the button to select the first record. Of course, he's expecting to hear his music. Rock and roll, man. Instead it's some kind of monotonous big band music. Try as he might, he can't get this lame music to stop playing. It's driving him crazy.

An old farmer appears, sitting in a rocking chair. Our guy asks the farmer what he thinks about The Beatles breaking up their band. The old farmer starts rambling on about boric acid being the best way to get rid of beetles. The guy can't stand it. When he thinks it can't get any worse, a couple, apparently just back from vacation, appears. Beside them is a projector with what looks like no less than a million slides of their trip to Tijuana.

He's over all of this and demands to see the Devil. When the Devil appears, he's nothing like our guy has imagined he would be. He decides to ask the Devil what happened to all his stuff. You know, things like whips and chains. What about the snakes or the boiling oil? These are the things the guy believes hell should have. The Devil explains that hell is never what it is expected to be. He goes on to tell the poor guy that this is it for him. He explains that there is also a room just like this one is in heaven. He tells the guy that although this room is hell for him, it's heaven to someone else. The Devil tells him to think about it. Then bids him farewell.

Hell's latest victim is now stuck in an atmosphere of eternal boredom, never to be a part of his cool and happening life again. In an effort to block out the tedious band music and the constant yapping of the vacationers and the farmer, our guy covers his ears with his hands. Unfortunately, it doesn't work. Hell has arrived. There's no escape.

So, where or what is hell for each of us? We all possess our own vision or version of hell. Some believe that we're currently living in hell on earth. I guess for some that could actually be true. When I see pictures or videos of people in other countries—or in our own country even—starving or living in inhumane conditions, I can see hell reflected in their faces. Documentaries that show people strung out on all sorts of drugs and/or alcohol have that look of hell pouring out through their pores. Stories about the mentally ill show that crazed look of hell. I'm sure the list could go on. Everyone knows there are times when we feel as though we're living in hell. I know I've gone through dark days like that.

When we find ourselves living in sadness, John 14:1–4 tells us about when Jesus was comforting His disciples: "Do not let your hearts be troubled. You believe in God; believe also in me. My Father's house has many rooms; if that were not so, would I have told you that I am going there to prepare a place for you? And if I go and prepare a place for you, I will come back and take you to be with me that you also may be where I am. You know the way to the place where I am going." Just reading those verses would make anyone feel better.

Fear is one of our biggest challenges as humans. It causes us to make bad decisions; it makes us foolish. It causes us to be unkind or filled with anger and hate. All the while, fear gives us a compelling need to find security. Psalm 121:1–8 is one of my favorite parts of the Bible. It speaks directly to fear and our never-ending need for security, as it reads: "I lift up my eyes to the mountains—where does my help come from? My help comes from the Lord, the Maker of heaven and earth. He will not let your foot slip—he who watches over you will not slumber; indeed, he who watches over Israel will neither slumber nor sleep. The Lord watches over you—the Lord is your shade at your right hand; the sun will not harm you by day, nor the moon by night. The Lord will keep you from all harm—he will watch over your life; the Lord will watch over your coming and going both now and forevermore." You gotta admit that deserves an Amen!

In the *Night Gallery* episode, the main character in his hell is pretty funny. Mainly because we're glad we're not that guy. We know that life is filled with moments which make us feel we're in hell. When we're years past the moment, we look back and wonder why those circumstances made us so crazy. We might even laugh.

Most situations where people feel like they are in the depths of hell are centered on family. Family functions come to mind when we think of hell. Holidays, reunions, and dividing the family inheritance are all situations where hell raises its ugly head. Even the annual family vacation can bring on hellacious anxiety. Ever get caught at the annual family reunion in between Aunt Martha and Uncle Joe, who both suffer from every disease known to man and feel the need to tell everyone within hearing distance all about every one of their ailments? Been there, right? We've all been there.

Let's consider family vacations. What can I say? Driving hundreds of miles with these people, we suddenly wonder what we ever saw in any of them. We wonder who they really are. How we can get away from them. We begin to plot against them in an effort to rid ourselves of their presence.

How about blind dates? Remember those? Jobs where a tyrant boss makes every day of work a day you'd rather stay home? Bumper-to-bumper traffic…early morning…after two cups of coffee…the exit with the bathroom is two miles away and all the cars have been sitting in the same spot for at least thirty minutes? It's that hell thing I tell you!

Then there are the many times we get out of bed and from that moment until we get back in bed that night, the entire day is a living hell. It looks something like this: we drop everything we touch, bump our head a hundred times, hit our knee on our desk drawer, trip every time we get up to walk, get thousands of paper cuts, choke on our tea and it comes out our nose. How about when you go to pay for lunch only to find you've left your wallet on your desk? Or when you decide to have a late afternoon cup of coffee which you promptly spill down the front of your *white* shirt and you have a dinner meeting scheduled? Then, of course, you go to your car to discover your battery is dead.

I remember a time when I left work late thinking I'd get home quickly because rush hour had ended only to find a five-car wreck on the freeway with bumper-to-bumper traffic. I'd not gone to the bathroom before leaving work and the exit with the bathroom was at least three exits away. One word—hell!

Many situations seem like hell but, when recounted, are truly funny. I believe that hell on earth can be a reality. It can also be a state of mind. Nevertheless, we experience serious times of feeling we are in hell. Those are the times our faith brings us full circle. We look back and see how we've grown, reflect on what we've learned because we've become survivors of that hell.

Then we experience those comical times when we feel we're in hell. Those are the times that give us that bit of a chuckle when recalled. No matter how we view hell, I can stand proudly and say unequivocally that I have seen hell, and I don't want to go there!

Chapter Nine

JUST HOW MUCH ARE YOU INVESTED IN YOUR DECISION?

REGINA STONE MATTHEWS

*I*NVESTMENTS CAN MAKE US OR BREAK US. THE WORD ITSELF is enough to make the strongest shake in his boots. It can even make grown men cry. Certainly, the world of investments is not for the weak at heart. My knowledge of investments, stocks, bonds, and the like would not even register on a Richter scale. To put it bluntly: I know nothing. Bulls? Bears? What? Sounds like something from a zoo. It makes my head spin. I do know, however, the old investment proverb that warns all who dare dabble in the world of investments: "buy on the rumor—sell on the news." The term means absolutely nothing to me other than it just sounds smart. Even looking up the phrase didn't help. No light-bulb moment that made me any more knowledgeable than before.

The word *investment* carries with it several definitions. We know it primarily means making a commitment of your time or your support. Remember those words—time and support. We'll be looking at them in a few minutes. Investment means devoting your talents or your energy, be it physical or emotional. All this *investment* is ultimately to achieve something.

Then there's the word *invest*. As in putting your money into something in order to make more money. Sweet, right? But only if it works out to that end. Seems investors need nerves of steel. Like gamblers, they're both in it for the money. Gamblers play to win. They take chances in order to turn a profit. An investor does much the same. But the investor has a little more information to go on than just a gut feeling or luck. Investors research before taking the plunge. They educate themselves to the world of investing as they soak up facts and figures of the things they find financially appealing.

But both the gambler and the investor never take their eyes off the ball. Doing so ends in a loss.

Most investors would never think of King Solomon as a role model, but that's exactly what he was. From what I've learned about him over the years, I'd appoint him as the best who ever lived when it came to the game of investing. One might even call him a giant. All in all, he took in close to twenty-five tons of gold on an annual basis. That sounds like a lot! According to the Bible, the amount of gold he made on an annual basis didn't even include the amount of money he took in from his merchants or from trading. He acquired income from other areas, also.

But don't take my word for it. Here is how 1 Kings 10:14–15 puts it: "The weight of the gold that Solomon received yearly was 666 talents, not including the revenues from merchants and traders and from all the Arabian kings and the governors of the territories." The Bible calls it *Solomon's Splendor*. Gotta love that. That 666 talents is about 25 tons or about 23 metric tons. Even the Queen of Sheba seemed impressed with how well King Solomon could turn a buck. How everything he touched turned to gold. If King Solomon lived today, he'd be worth in excess of a billion dollars. Maybe more. That's without using a computer or the daily stock exchange information sheets. Pretty impressive.

Now for the rub. King Solomon, in all his wisdom and good fortune, made some blunders along the way. His father, King David, warned him before his own death that he (Solomon) should always stay in fellowship with God and never break God's commandments. King David's instructions appear in 1 Kings 2:2–4: "I am about to go the way of all the earth," he said. "So be strong, act like a man, and observe what the Lord your God requires: Walk in obedience to him, and keep his decrees and commands, his laws and regulations, as written in the Law of Moses. Do this so that you may prosper in all you do and wherever you go and that the Lord may keep his promise to me: 'If your descendants watch how they live, and if they walk faithfully before me with all their heart and soul, you will never fail to have a successor on the throne of Israel.'"

The obvious question is, did he listen? The answer is, well, kinda/sorta. Sounds a lot like my kids! Solomon definitely loved God. His father told him to *walk* with God. Not just to love Him. Not just to obey Him. King David wanted more for his son. Solomon, on the other hand, figured it was okay if he did things like other people as long as he loved God, too. So instead of *walking* with God, he walked with *people*. Never a good plan.

In summary, God decided to give Solomon a wakeup call. It made a point. Solomon asked God to give him wisdom so that he would be equipped to tell good from evil. Solomon's response to God's tapping him on the shoulder appears in 1 Kings 3:9–10: '"So give your servant a discerning heart to govern your people and to distinguish between right and wrong. For who is able to govern this great people of yours?' The Lord was pleased that Solomon had asked for this." That's what you call the *key* to everything, particularly when it comes to investing or making decisions. The ability to tell right from wrong gives us the ability to make good decisions whether they be in investing or other areas. I submit that Solomon knew this all along. He knew that God blessed him with this ability, which led to King Solomon being the greatest investor who ever lived.

Now, here's the *however* and *even though* parts of the story of King Solomon. *Even though* God gave Solomon all this wisdom, Solomon, in my opinion, got a little too big for his britches. He decided that in all his wisdom he would walk with God only when it was convenient for him to walk with God. Well, God don't play that way. Unfortunately for Solomon, he liked women a little too much. He possessed (don't get crazy about that word—it's how it went down at that time) seven hundred wives, princesses, and three hundred concubines. Not a very good formula for success. Nevertheless, Solomon found himself invested in this type of lifestyle. Soon, he allowed all his wives to turn his heart away from God. His father, David, on the other hand, devoted himself wholly to God.

Consequences followed. In 1 Kings 11:9–13 we read: "The Lord became angry with Solomon because his heart had turned away from the Lord, the God of Israel, who had appeared to him twice. Although he had forbidden Solomon to follow other gods, Solomon did not keep the Lord's command. So the Lord said to Solomon, 'Since this is your attitude and you have not kept my covenant and my decrees, which I commanded you, I will most certainly tear the kingdom away from you and give it to one of your subordinates. Nevertheless, for the sake of David your father, I will not do it during your lifetime. I will tear it out of the hand of your son. Yet I will not tear the whole kingdom from him, but will give him one tribe for the sake of David my servant and for the sake of Jerusalem, which I have chosen.'"

In his old age, Solomon realized that even though he possessed all this wisdom, all this fame, all this fortune, he possessed nothing because he decided to walk with people instead of walking with God. Being invested in one's decisions can bring with it some severe consequences.

The Bible contains definitions of words. In the book of Ecclesiastes 11:1–2, we read one definition of the word investment. Likewise in Proverbs 15:22, Luke 16:11, and Matthew 6:21. In Proverbs 21:20 we read my favorite definition of investment: "The wise store up choice food and olive oil, but fools gulp theirs down."

One of the best stories about investments is when Jesus tells the Parable of the Talents. It's a compelling story about three men and their abilities to turn a profit for their master. Check it out in the twenty-fifth chapter of Matthew.

When we make decisions, naturally we have a need to weigh our options. That's basically how decisions are made. We depend mostly on ourselves. But the Bible describes "decision" differently in Proverbs 3:5–6: "Trust in the Lord with all your heart and lean not on your own understanding; in all your ways submit to him, and he will make your paths straight." Whereas words like "making up one's own mind" might be more popular or more empowering, the Bible tells us to trust in the *Lord*, and *He* will guide us toward the right decision. That amounts to faith. But faith is difficult at best when making a decision. We all want to believe we are in control of our decisions. But then don't we all want to be in control of most everything? We invest our all into our decisions, fighting to the end to defend them. Tell that to Moses. Tell it to Abraham. Tell it to Noah. They all made decisions based on nothing more than faith.

The investment we put into our decision is precious to us. Any threat or criticism toward that decision is met with one's back fully up.

The biggest problem we face when making a decision is knowing we might be wrong. What if this decision we are getting ready to make turns out to be the biggest mistake of our lives? What if this decision hurts or even costs the life of someone? What if the decisions we've made throughout our life have all been the wrong ones?

Investing so much in a decision tends to make people defensive. Some go so far as to covet their own decisions. Usually the first person to realize a decision is wrong is the person making the decision. Admitting it out loud will most likely never happen. Unfortunately, the first person to call attention to the wrong decision is someone else. Herein lies the dilemma.

Ever confront someone who has clearly made a wrong decision? So, how did that play out? Bad, I'm guessing. We've invested so much in our decisions that sometimes we become blind to the realities that lay before us. What makes it even worse, we dig in our heels so deeply that we become unreasonable. Admitting a wrong decision is the last thing anyone wants to do. In our efforts to avoid that, we begin the blame game. We start pointing fingers so as not to assume responsibility for making the wrong decision in the first place. It then becomes a vicious circle.

So, here we are at the point of a decision. Remember those words *time* and *support* that were used earlier when defining investment? When decisions are made, we invest so much of our time that, either admitting the decision was wrong or needing to defend our decision, flies in our face. Why? Who wants to waste time? It's like being robbed or having property vandalized. We invest our time, also known as our life, into what we have. When what we've worked for is taken from us or destroyed, it's devastating. Not just for the things but for the time it took to get the things. The sweat of our brow means something. Time equals life, equals effort, equals investment.

Now, how about that word *support*? When we make decisions, do we not want to be supported in that decision? After all, we just spent all this time investing in the decision itself. Without support, the decision becomes wobbly. How does a person deal with that? Support is a valuable commodity. All decisions require it. It's needed to sustain our decision. To justify the investment.

Additionally, the emotional energy that's invested in a decision is a big deal. I bet most of us value emotional energy more than we value physical energy. Emotional energy drains every inch of us. Healing from physical exhaustion is much easier than healing from emotional exhaustion. Therefore, decisions that are made through the investment of time and emotional energy make us hell-bound to stick to our guns when confronted with the possibility of making the wrong decision. Defensiveness is a great mechanism.

Decisions, good or bad, are simply decisions. I guess they're a lot like stocks and bonds. Sometimes the decisions we make are on a high. Sometimes the decisions we make bring on a low. No matter how we get to those decisions throughout our lives, get there we must. We all face difficult decisions at some point. Some we would really rather not make. True character, in my mind, is when we can logically look at a decision we've made and say, "It was the wrong decision." That's not a weakness. That's true strength.

As I look back at my own decisions, I can honestly say I made some good ones. I can also honestly say I made some pretty dumb ones. Investment paid a huge role in those decisions, good or bad. Now I ask you? Just how much are *you* invested in your decisions?

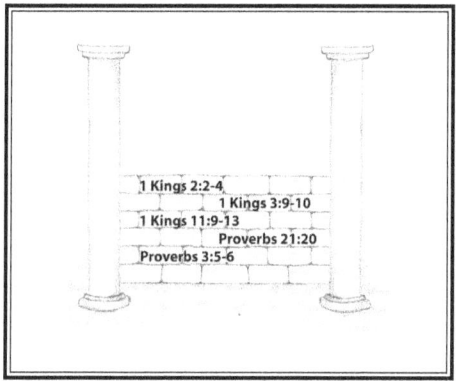

Chapter Ten

LOWERING OF THE BAR

A PLACE CALLED *Common Sense*

*A*s a child, I really hated history. This drove my parents crazy because they believed history to be the cornerstone of our learning. My mother taught fifth grade before I totally disrupted her life. She taught history. My daddy served in the military and in two wars. History meant a lot to him. They drove me crazy with history pop-quizzes. Consequently, I learned, and I remembered. The bar was set pretty high for me with a mother who taught history and a daddy who served in the military. Now, I love history. I'm not an expert, mind you. But I enjoy learning as much as I can.

In remembrance of my mother and daddy, I pose this history pop-quiz: How many signatures appear on the Declaration of Independence? Give up? Fifty-six. Know anything about the men behind the signatures? Like, what they did for a living? Know what happened to all those guys? Well, some went on to do great things. Some stayed in politics in a quiet way, not doing anything spectacular, just serving the people. Reports indicate that there were lawyers and jurists along with merchants, farmers, and large plantation owners. All who signed the Declaration did so through great sacrifice. These brave men literally risked everything for the cause of freedom. They fulfilled every commitment, living up to the highest of expectations. I'd say the bar was set exceptionally high at that time in history.

Exactly how far have we lowered the bar in the last decade? I would imagine quite a bit. It seems as though in every year that passes by, we lower that bar just a little more. Over the years of my life, the bar seems to have gone from way over my head to just below my knees. As more technology becomes available to the public, along with radio and TV stations spewing out non-stop information, we can actually see the bar going down.

I submit that entitlements are a huge reason this is happening. When people are given more, it takes away their reason to work. When their reason to work is gone, their pride weakens. When their pride is gone, they become dependent. When a person's independence no longer exists, we then take away their reason for living.

The proof is in the number of homeless, drug addicted, runaways, and prostitutes. Sadly, it's the laziness that's defining society. Even though we're keenly aware of the situations that surround us, we do nothing in an effort to raise the bar.

Sad to think we have very few in our body of government who would sacrifice in the way our founders did. We find ourselves making excuses for a government that finds more value in the power or prestige of the office instead of fulfilling the role of representatives "of the people, for the people and by the people." Before long, we decide we can do nothing about the people who represent our interests, so we just accept it. And the bar drops a little lower.

Remember the old Chinese Proverb about giving a man a fish? It goes like this, "Give a man a fish and you feed him for a day. Teach a man to fish, and you feed him for a lifetime." People seem to forget that logic. In order to earn, one must work. We don't need entitlements. Only politicians need us to need entitlements. What we need is to know what is expected of us. If we expect something of someone, we look to the likelihood that it will happen. We anticipate or expect that the person will do as he or she committed to do. Expectations and commitments go hand-in-hand.

Most of us expect people to live up to their commitments.

When they don't, we're disappointed. Whether or not people who disappoint even care is a non-issue because they aren't the ones feeling the slap in the face that disappointment often brings. After a while, we decide we can do nothing about it. And the bar drops a little lower.

As this country has aged, we've fallen into a dream-state whereby we drift through life noticing only those things that lull us into a state of euphoria. Less pain that way. "Expectations" isn't *really* what it means. It's a kinda/sorta take on the word. Its true definition speaks to the probability that something will actually occur. That certainly doesn't sound like something one would want hanging over their head. What could possibly be worse than having someone *expect* something of us? Expectations can really get in the way of our leisure time.

The Bible speaks very specifically about expectations. In particular it speaks to God's expectations of us, as we read in Hebrews 10:26–27: "If we deliberately keep on sinning after we have received the knowledge of the truth, no sacrifice for sins is left, but only a fearful expectation of judgment and of raging fire that will consume the enemies of God."

Maybe it's just me, but I believe we should have certain expectations of those around us. People we work with, people we're friends with, and in particular the people we call family. We expect our co-workers to be honest, hard-working. We expect our friends to be loyal, trustworthy. We expect our family to love us unconditionally. To be there for us in our times of need. Unfortunately, expectations have a way of leading to disappointment. Before long, we decide we can do nothing about the fact that people don't fulfill our expectations, so we just accept it. And the bar drops a little lower.

Then that "commitment" word comes along, and we

all head for the hills. I've actually seen grown men break into a sweat followed by hives at the mere mention of the word "commitment." My guess is because it requires an obligation or even engagement. Very scary stuff. We don't really need commitments in our lives, do we? Can't we just say that we'll try—try our best—try our hardest? Isn't that really all anyone can do?

Here's how the Bible sees that in Numbers 30:1–2: "Moses said to the heads of the tribes of Israel: 'This is what the Lord commands: When a man makes a vow to the Lord or takes an oath to obligate himself by a pledge, he must not break his word but must do everything he said.'" Oh my, there are those scary words again.

I would conclude that making a commitment would be considered a very serious act. Nevertheless, we tend to water it down by committing just a little. It's okay if we don't commit all the way. Or maybe we'll commit then pretend we really didn't commit. It's just too hard to always keep a commitment. Extenuating circumstances and all. Yeah, that's what it is. Those extenuating circumstances. Then before long we decide that we can do nothing about the fact that people just don't follow through with their commitments, so we accept it. And the bar drops a little lower.

The lowering of the bar doesn't just apply to our government. It applies to our workplaces, as well. We find our workplace inundated with those who have no regard for their co-workers. Covering one's derriere is the norm. Not standing up for rights, just yielding to wrongs. Consequently, we just decide we can do nothing about the workplace or the people who run them. Before long we just accept it. And the bar drops a little lower.

Then there are the children. I don't know what breaks my heart more: the condition of a country I hold dear or the condition of its children. A generation of kids who are breastfed on entitlements. I've known for a long time that each generation experiences some form of deterioration. With each generation, we see children stepping further into complacency. They possess no sense of urgency. Duty or honor mean very little. We rear children to believe they don't need to fail. They watch as our government encourages entitlements. And, they learn.

Now don't get me wrong, I'm not all doom-and-gloom about the kids of today. I know there are kids out there who do magnificent things. I even founded a *Kids Inspiring Kids* site. I'm not referring to those kids. I'm referring to the ones who show up on YouTube beating the snot out of each other, or those who show up on TV beating the snot out of some elderly person or rioting and looting in the streets. Or the ones who need safe zones because they feel offended or threatened.

Looking at it for what it really is will show that young people are getting further away from what is righteous, turning more toward what is impious. Three philosophers spoke of the children of their time. One said, "What is happening to our young people? They disrespect their elders, they disobey their parents. They ignore the law. They riot in the streets inflamed with wild notions. Their morals are decaying. What is to become of them?" That was Plato, born around 428-427 BC.

The next philosopher said, "I see no hope for the future of our people if they are dependent on the frivolous youth of today, for certainly all youth are reckless beyond words. When I was young, we were taught to be discreet and respectful of elders, but the present youth are exceedingly wise (disrespectful) and impatient of restraint." That one was Hesiod who lived in 8th century BC.

The final philosopher said, "The children now love luxury. They have bad manners, contempt for authority, they show disrespect to their elders. They no longer rise when elders enter the room. They contradict their parents, chatter before company, gobble up dainties at the table, cross their legs, and are tyrants over their teachers." That was Socrates who was born between 469 and 470 BC. So, I guess fearing for the children has been going on for quite a while.

One might argue that these quotes negate my point that the children of this generation are one step further away from knowing what it means to honor anything. Not so. Although each generation is met with the worry of the preceding generation, we find that along with that concern is the reality of the technology of today. What it brings to our children. Although the philosophers of the centuries before Christ spoke of their young people much in the same way as we do today, the difference was the expectations. Their bar was set so very high that the strictness and discipline of the time made the least little rebellion stick out.

Today we coddle, excuse, or befriend, never parenting or leading by example. We allow the children to run the household instead of the parents running the children. We tire of the constant battle. Before long we just decide we can do nothing about the children anyway. Just go with the flow. Hold your breath until they grow up and hopefully move out. We simply accept it. And the bar drops a little lower.

Where do we go from here? Good question. Attempting to raise the bar might be a start. Leading by example, keeping our commitments, not giving up on expectations can help. How about bringing back the meaning of the words *respect* and *honor*? Remembering that there is no shame in failing, only shame in not trying? To think that a country, its people, as great as they once were, as great as they can be, would sit around on their laurels all the while allowing the bar to drop so very low is not only sad but maddening.

I've often wondered what the Founding Fathers would think of their nation at this point in time. My guess is they would be ashamed. They would most likely tell us that this was not what they saw unfolding when they wrote the *Declaration of Independence* and *The Constitution*. Then they would probably cry.

So here's a word of warning—or a word to the wise, as my grandfather used to say. It appears in 2 Timothy 3:1–5: "But mark this: There will be terrible times in the last days. People will be lovers of themselves, lovers of money, boastful, proud, abusive, disobedient to their parents, ungrateful, unholy, without love, unforgiving, slanderous, without self-control, brutal, not lovers of the good, treacherous, rash, conceited, lovers of pleasure rather than lovers of God—having a form of godliness but denying its power. Have nothing to do with such people." Strong language but necessary.

Ephesians 4:1–3 just might put all of this into perspective: "As a prisoner for the Lord, then, I urge you to live a life worthy of the calling you have received. Be completely humble and gentle; be patient, bearing with one another in love. Make every effort to keep the unity of the Spirit through the bond of peace."

When we lower the bar to a point whereby we see no wrong in the wrong we are doing, well, we better watch out, because before long, we decide we can do nothing about it. So we just accept it, and the bar drops a little lower.

I've always admired military courtesy. Saluting a commanding officer is a core expression of respect for authority in the military world. Being an Army brat, I found courtesy burned into my brain. All the "yes sirs/no sirs," "yes ma'ams/no ma'ams," "please sirs/ma'ams," "thank you sirs/ma'ams," became a permanent part of my vocabulary. It set standards that caused me to show respect for others.

When I'm out and see a soldier, I always say, "Thank you." You don't even have to follow it by saying, "for your service." They know by the tone in your voice. They never fail to acknowledge with either a nod of the head or a verbal, "You're welcome." They always smile.

These are the simple things done in an effort to prevent the lowering of the bar.

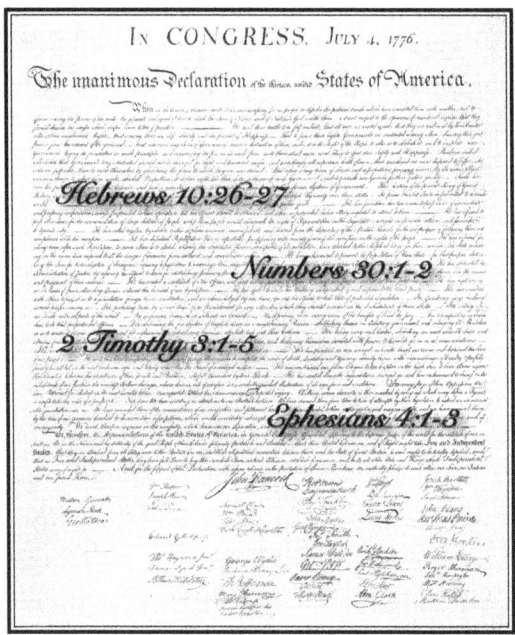

Chapter Eleven

NEVER JUDGE A BOOK BY ITS COVER

*O*NCE UPON A TIME THERE WAS THIS THING CALLED *The Golden Rule*. It spoke to fairness, compassion, consideration, empathy, humaneness, kindness, mercy, and grace. We're taught these things. If we're not taught them, we know about them. Some choose to ignore them. We don't always *do unto others as we would have others do unto us.*

The legal system teaches that *a man is innocent until proven guilty*. Some choose to ignore that as well. An unknown author wrote, *Treat everyone with politeness, even those who are rude to you—not because they are nice, but because you are.* Should we heed these offerings, we'd never judge a book by its cover again.

I went through elementary school being bullied by kids who didn't like the fact that my parents were both of Cherokee Indian descent. In the late 1950s to early 1960s (my elementary school years) being from any descent that didn't carry the name of white Anglo was a big deal and detrimental to your well-being, both mentally and physically. My mother taught school but stopped teaching after I was born to stay home with me. When I started school, she began to substitute teach. Somehow the parents at the local school discovered her heritage and petitioned the school not to allow her to teach. God was ever present that day because the principal stood his ground. He denied the petition and allowed my mother to teach. So I became the target. At the beginning, it frightened me. I never told my parents because my dad (part Cherokee/part Irish—a deadly combination) would have taken his tomahawk to those kids. I felt it would only make matters worse.

I think my parents knew all along, which meant they were much cooler than I gave them credit for because they never intervened. Instead my daddy taught me how to defend myself, which ultimately gave me the confidence I needed to stand up to the bullying. You see, bullies are really just cowards. They never meet you one-on-one. They always approach you in a pack. Understand, the Internet and social networking didn't exist in the 1950s–1960s. A kid got bullied face-to-face, and it usually became physical. In today's world, bullies are much the same—cowards. Now they hide behind the Internet so they don't have to travel in packs. And the cuts are deeper, I think.

I remember a contestant on a talent show who made me think not only about bullying but about judging a book by its cover. She did it by simply walking on stage, opening her mouth, and singing. The crowd's reaction to her left a bitter taste in my mouth. It reminded me of a girl I once knew whose appearance didn't rise to the level of pretty. In fact, a lot of people called her ugly to her face. We became friends, and I used to cry for her when others called her names. I remember actually punching a kid in the nose for his hatefulness. It gave me great satisfaction. She, however, encouraged me to control my anger. Although I tried, I failed more times than I succeeded. I know she handled those times much better than I did.

I found it interesting that the contestant chose the song "I Dreamed a Dream" to sing. The lyrics of the song are truly gut-wrenching. If you look them up, you'll notice you can't read them aloud without choking up. It's even more difficult to hear them sung.

A bit of a setup to the song is in order. *Les Miserables* is a novel written by Victor Hugo in 1862. Most know about *Les Miserables* through its many stage and screen adaptations.

Fantine is the character in the musical adaptation of the novel who sings "I Dreamed a Dream."

Fantine is this poor soul abandoned by the man she loved, the man who fathered her child, Cosette. When her employer discovers she's an unwed mother, she's terminated. She then turns to prostitution. Alone and destitute, Fantine sings the incredible song, "I Dreamed a Dream."

The song speaks of a time when people were kind and spoke to each other softly with words of comfort. Fantine is painfully aware of the fact that once upon a time the world flowed with joy like a beautiful song. Those who loved saw no ugliness because love, as we know, is blind. Fantine makes the claim that because all went wrong, the world is no longer the place she remembers. She goes on to speak of a time that no longer exists—a time of hope coupled with the pleasure of living. She dreams of when her hopes were high, when love seemed a forever thing, when God would always forgive.

She reminds herself of her youth and the fearlessness that goes with it. With that fearlessness comes hazards. She recalls how we make dreams only to waste them because we all believe, when we're young, that we will never have to pay the price for living frivolously. Unaware of what the future held, Fantine discovers that life has a way of quietly turning on you, ripping every bit of hope away. Turning any dream you might possess into a shameful waste.

As the song goes on, Fantine remembers how the man she loved so deeply betrayed her, taking away her innocence. Then he slipped away into the night without a word. She still wants him back. She dreams that someday he will return. That they will live happily ever after. All the while knowing in her heart of hearts that there are dreams we hold close that can never come true. She fears there will be times in her life when she will not be able to stand the pain. In the end, she sees her life as wasted. She never imagined things would turn out so badly. Because of how life has beaten her down, she comes to the conclusion that her dream is dead.

Okay, so I'm blubbering. How about you? If we think back, we find that the contestant, as well as my friend, were both judged harshly by their peers. We do it as children. We do it as adults. In a world that preaches political correctness, I find this extraordinary. In the end, the contestant did exceptionally well, astonishing everyone in the house with her amazing voice. She touched the hearts of millions. As for my friend, well, she never became famous, but she became someone I loved dearly and tremendously respected.

Cruelty certainly has no conscience. It crosses all ethnic boundaries. It breeds throughout societies whose goal it is to defame those who don't fit into a preconceived idea of perfection. We see it also when we disagree on certain subjects. People are vilified for their points of view if they aren't part of the mainstream. I'm ashamed to admit I've fallen into the category of cruelty at some point in my lifetime.

We can find no greater guide for how to treat one another than God's Word. Ephesians 4:32 tells us: "Be kind and compassionate to one another, forgiving each other, just as in Christ God forgave you." Challenging to say the least. To be kind to *everyone*? To forgive *everyone*? Not easy. Forgiveness is probably my biggest obstacle in life.

Then in 1 Peter 3:8 we read: "Finally, all of you, be likeminded, be sympathetic, love one another, be compassionate and humble." Now for the knockout punch in Matthew 7:1–2: "Do not judge, or you too will be judged. For in the same way you judge others, you will be judged, and with the measure you use, it will be measured to you."

How we handle ridicule or cruelty reveals the person we are inside. Would we dare forgive? Would we even dare show kindness in return?

There *was* a time when men were kind and love was blind. I'm certain of it. Cruelty, as well as cynicism, both have strong roots. But it's not a mistake or a dream that God is forgiving. He must be. Look at what He deals with every day. My hope is that life will not kill the dream any one of us dares to dream.

There are those among us who make us realize that grace comes in all packages. That turning the other cheek is a trait too few possess. That the Golden Rule can really be practiced. Consequently, when we encounter those people, we understand we should never judge a book by its cover.

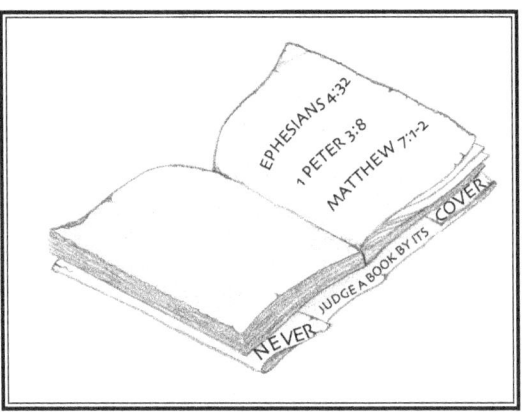

Chapter Twelve

SO, ARE YOU HAVING FUN IN YOUR PURSUIT OF HAPPINESS? THAT'S THE QUESTION

REGINA STONE MATTHEWS

*O*NE SUMMER WHILE VISITING MY DAUGHTER, SHE SHOWED me the movie *The Pursuit of Happyness*. I will probably never forgive her for it. We were just hanging out eating M & M's (never a healthy thing to do but so much fun) when this evil child of mine asks if I'd ever seen this movie. I had not. She goes on to tell me how much I'm going to love it. How inspiring it is. What a huge statement it makes in regards to determination and hard work—all those things I told her about during her childhood and hoped they'd stick. During her gymnastic days, I told her this sport would test her. How it could suck the life out of her unless she remained determined and not afraid of hard work. So how could I not want to watch this movie with her? Did I mention I'll probably never forgive her?

I make that statement because the story wore me down to the bone. By the end of this thing, I found myself completely exhausted, both mentally and physically. My makeup dissolved because I cried almost from the beginning right through to the end. Exhausted, also, from screaming at the guy's loser wife, all the people trying to steal his machines, and the schmuck who taught the stockbroker class. Let me just make this very important point: the lead role was cast perfectly.

The movie is based on the true-life story of Chris Gardner. Thanks to my daughter, who is no longer in my will, I've now probably watched it over a hundred times, crying in all the same places, yelling at all the same people, swearing never to watch it again—until I do.

In all the times I'd watched it, however, I'd never noticed how the word "happiness" was spelled in the actual title until just recently. In the movie, the Chris Gardner character keeps pointing his son's attention to the word *happyness* written on a wall outside of the babysitter's house. Happiness was misspelled. The kid didn't care, but his father showed it to him every time, each time explaining how it should be spelled.

Then one day while working out (I put that in to impress) and watching the movie yet again, when the title of the movie came on the screen, I said to myself, "I've never seen that **Y** in that word before!" The title read, *The Pursuit of* **Happyness.** It's amazing how the eyes work. You see a word you've seen for years. You know how it's spelled. You know how to pronounce it. Someone changes one letter, and it never registers. At least it never registered with me as it might have with most. It took me a while, but it finally clicked.

If you're familiar with an essay entitle "Liberty Further Extended," written by Lemuel Haynes, you'll notice that the misspelling of the word happiness came from that essay. Haynes lived in New England during the Revolution. Abandoned by his mother, a Caucasian, and his father, an African, at the age of five months, he was handed over to indentured servitude, a form of debt bondage or slavery. Fortunately, educating him was part of the agreement. Around the age of twenty, he witnessed the Aurora Borealis, which scared the life out of him. He thought it meant the beginning of the end of the world, so he immediately found Jesus. After that he joined the Minutemen. Then, after the American Revolution, he began writing. When he wrote his essay, he quoted Thomas Jefferson's sentence in the *Declaration of Independence* but spelled the word **happyness** instead of **happiness.**

When we think of happiness, we typically think emotion. If talking with a philosopher, then happiness might be defined as "living the good life." Most people would probably define it as pleasure. Some may even see it as well-being, quality of life, or even fame. There are a million definitions for it, I'm sure. In the movie, the main character says, "How did he (Thomas Jefferson) know to put that word "pursuit" in there?"

Did he mean we can never acquire or obtain happiness? Beats me. I'd never really thought about it that way because I've always known throughout my life the times when I experienced happiness. There were also times when it was nowhere in sight. I never felt it to be a right.

While on my treadmill that day, watching that gut-wrenching movie that my now disinherited daughter made me watch, I had an epiphany. There's actually an **I** in happiness. That's why we all pursue it. It's all for the **I**. What a bunch of selfish, self-centered, self-absorbed, egotistical, people we all are. Except for me. Not really. But it's okay to want happiness for oneself. The challenge is how one pursues it. Some pursue it honestly and legally; some don't. It depends on the type person.

So, during our pursuit of happiness, do we concentrate on the **I** or do we concentrate on the **Y**. The **Y** seems to represent the **You** in our lives—meaning someone other than ourselves. Either Lemuel Haynes was a poor speller or simply a good guy. He actually became a minister sometime during the 1780s. Overall, he preached equality, which is always a good thing as long as it's not taken to the extreme or manipulated. For that I applaud his passion. Makes you think the **Y** might not have been a mistake on his part after all.

As I look at my own pursuit of happiness, I see the glass half full in that I believe those of us who have children are more concerned with the **Y**. We work all of our lives to feed these people, to clothe them, to put them through school, to put a roof over their head. What do we get in return? Grief! Oh, sorry, that would be another rant. In all seriousness, we do these things because we love them. We want the best for them. Somewhere along the line we lose sight of our own happiness and focus on the happyness of our children. Of course, there are some who never lose sight of their own happiness. These people are called politicians. So not kidding! There certainly are non-political people who focus on themselves. I believe they're called everyday people. They strive for the pursuit of happiness to the extreme. Living only for the **I**. There's no **Y** for them in their world.

When I look at people who are desperately in pursuit of happiness, the first thing that comes to my mind is, "So, why are they not happy?" They pursue a career, money, fame, power, and one another until happiness is found in the pursuit instead of any accomplishment. During all of this pursuing, they've missed life. One then must wonder, was it worth it? Did they get what they wanted in the end? I'm not so sure. If happiness is only a pursuit, why bother? Because like the main character of *The Pursuit of Happyness* said, "How did he know to put the word "pursuit" in there?" It certainly sounds unobtainable. Maybe the **I** is important after all.

My granddaughter is in love with a certain group of young men who sing. When she reads this, I'm pretty sure I'll be out of *her* will, but I must mention this nevertheless. It escapes me which one in the group she loves the best, but I know there's one that causes her heart to sputter more than the others. I decided to check these kids out because I'm quite confident none of them are good enough for my granddaughter. I came away thinking, cute, but singing? I found a video. As I viewed it a second time, I turned down the sound just to watch. Then I cried.

Let's take a walk down memory lane, where the streets are lined with the likes of Frank Sinatra, Elvis Presley, The Beatles, The Rolling Stones, and The Beach Boys. I list these performers because of the mania they caused.

I can remember watching Elvis Presley when he appeared for the first time on TV on *The Ed Sullivan Show*. (And, yes, I am that old.) The show's producers had to shoot him from the waist up because the network considered the moving and shaking of his hips vulgar.

Then came the mania that surrounded the Beatles, also known as Beatle MANIA.

Long before that, we were introduced to Frank Sinatra, old blue eyes. The girls went crazy over this skinny little guy.

The Rolling Stones sailed around the Beatles. They're *still* rolling.

Finally, The Beach Boys with their California dreamboat looks and dreamy sounds.

When the camera pans out over the crowds at the concerts of these people, young women are crying, wringing their hands, jumping up and down, screaming, waving their arms in the air, eating their clothes. But the most pathetic of all are the ones reaching out toward the performer in an effort to touch them. Just once. Just one magical moment when their hand touches the hand of the performer.

As I watched the video, I saw the same mania. I immediately reflected back on others who traveled down that same road in the pursuit of happiness.

Certainly I don't know, nor did I ever know, any of these people personally. I possess no knowledge of what their personal lives are or were about. We all know what we know from the tabloids, the newspapers, or the gossip tell-all media, but we don't really know. I do imagine that their lives are lonely in the sense they can't just take a walk or go to the market or the mall without being mauled. That constitutes loneliness to me. There's that **I** again.

Ironically, in the video I saw three kids looking like they were having the time of their lives. They were the true definition of the word happiness. Reaching out to touch a young fan but not really touching her for fear they would be pulled into the crowd. Inviting a young girl on stage for a hug only to see her break down in tears over the simple gesture. Signing endless mounds of posters. Pulling up in a limo to the sound of screaming fans. Bodyguards. Playing in the snow alone. Walking off stage. More bodyguards. As a mere mortal, I look at this with angst because, for me, I wouldn't want that for my child.

Now for my granddaughter's sake, I'll stop dumping on these kids. Let's bring it down to an everyday world level. The pursuit of happiness is just that. It's a pursuit, right? The **I** and the **Y** *do* make a difference. In Psalm 1:1-3 we read: "Blessed is the one who does not walk in step with the wicked or stand in the way that sinners take or sit in the company of mockers, but whose delight is in the law of the Lord, and who meditates on his law day and night. That person is like a tree planted by streams of water, which yields its fruit in season and whose leaf does not wither—whatever they do prospers." To this simple mind, that's the true definition of the pursuit of happiness.

Look to the left. Now look to the right. Are you pursuing happiness or happyness? Should you stumble across it, you would recognize it? When you do find it, is it everything you thought it would be? Has the journey been worth it? In other words, are you having fun in your pursuit of happiness? That's the question.

Chapter Thirteen

STANDING IN THE SHADOW OF ROCKY BALBOA

REGINA STONE MATTHEWS

I LOVE THE SPORT OF BOXING. THERE, I SAID IT! PLEASE don't contact the local shrinks to give them my phone number. This is not a mental disorder, nor is it a severe character flaw. My Uncle Bennie introduced me to boxing. He also introduced me to wrestling, but I found myself more drawn to boxing.

I couldn't have been more than seven years old when Uncle Bennie thought it a good idea to have me watch a boxing match on TV. It dazzled me. Even at seven, I got it. Keep in mind that boxing matches aired on TV ended in 1960. It was a good run while it lasted. I couldn't tell you the exact match I saw for the first time. All I know is that it made an impression. I'd have to say that Muhammad Ali had the biggest impact on me. Most likely due to his flamboyant personality. But, let's face it, Ali could box. There were others— Sugar Ray Robinson, Sonny Liston, Floyd Patterson, and Archie Moore. All amazing fighters.

As to the fight that confirmed my love for the sport? It had to be Ali vs. Frazier, famously known as The Fight of the Century. Joe Frazier, the WBC/WBA heavyweight champion and *The Ring*/lineal heavyweight champion, Muhammad Ali. I was nineteen at the time. Almost an entire year out of high school. The fight took place at Madison Square Garden in NYC on March 8, 1971. Both boxers were undefeated. So, who won? Dare I tell you? Okay, Frazier! But the story didn't end there. You're just going to have to look it up to find out what I mean.

Ultimately, I love the sport of boxing for this reason: *personal internal strength*. It's a character trait that's embedded within one's soul. A person can't be a successful boxer without it. That doesn't mean any athlete can't step into the ring.

But without personal internal strength an up-and-coming boxer simply won't make it. Just ask any of the boxers who've known the defeat of a knock-out.

When I discovered James J. Braddock, another boxer who stirred my interest, I truly understood what it meant to possess this necessary trait. Braddock's personal internal strength shined through every part of his being. He was known to all as an honorable man. During the Great Depression, Braddock and his family lived in poverty. He had to give up boxing in order to work as a longshoreman. When the Depression came to an end and he returned to boxing, he returned the welfare money he'd received. Humiliated by having to take the money to begin with, he felt an obligation to return it when he began making good money.

Then the fight! Braddock versus Baer. Braddock, the underdog, won and became the Heavyweight Champion of the World. That's what made me really appreciate the talent and dedication of boxing. Although this particular fight took place in 1935, I read about it and watched the video of it. Plus, I remember my Uncle Benny loved Braddock and told me all about him. Talk about an amazing fight. Max Baer's claim to fame revolved around his one-two punch and the ability to knock out his opponent. But Braddock took his punches and won. And that solidified my boxing obsession.

Not only do I love the sport of boxing, I love Rocky Balboa. Please don't write me letters telling me that Rocky Balboa is fictitious. I know this. I love the Rocky Balboa character, and the character of Rocky Balboa. He possessed that personal internal strength as well. It set him apart. He never quit. He never gave up. He went the distance. He didn't stop until the bell rang. I know, I know, he quit once, but that was the only time. It happened with Clubber Lang. I never liked Clubber Lang anyway. What a punk.

Rocky didn't quit for very long. He came back. He had to. Quitting went against his grain as a fighter. His personal internal strength kicked in, with Clubber Lang paying the price.

The very first movie, *Rocky*, is my favorite. It showcased Rocky's personal internal strength. His opponent, Apollo Creed, didn't have it. Regardless of his title, his technique, his ability, his physical strength, he couldn't overcome his arrogance or his ego. When those two things are added together, they equal *vanity*, which, oddly enough, is one of the Seven Deadly Sins.

Here were two fighters—a nobody and a Champ. Rocky doesn't win in the first movie, but he goes the distance, something no other fighter ever accomplished with Apollo Creed. For the first time in his career, Apollo Creed came face-to-face with a force he couldn't easily conquer. Instead of reaching inward for personal internal strength, Creed reached outward, toward vanity, clinging to his ego. When the two met again, it cost him his title.

Any boxer will tell you that over-confidence—or underestimating your opponent—will kill you in the ring. All great fighters know this. Rocky knew it. Apollo Creed did not. So Creed became one of those standing in the shadow of Rocky Balboa.

There were other victims of Rocky's shadow. Take, for instance, his brother-in-law, Paulie. A total loser, but a loveable one. There's just no nice way to put it. Paulie blamed everybody for every circumstance that surrounded his life. "It's not my fault" became his theme song. He couldn't get out from under the shadow of Rocky Balboa. He tried—a little. But when it became too difficult, he quit. Paulie did that best. He blamed his sister, Adrian, for keeping him down. When Rocky became famous, he blamed Rocky for keeping him down. But he never hesitated to ask for something. He wanted to make money off Rocky's name. He wanted this or that but never really wanted to do the hard stuff to get it. Through it all, Rocky never abandoned him. Unfortunately for Paulie, he never really got out from under the shadow of Rocky Balboa.

The most poignant of all the victims of Rocky's shadow was his only son, Robert Balboa, Jr. (also known as Rocky, Jr.), who blamed not only his lousy life but his very existence on Rocky. Although I do love the first *Rocky* movie, the one entitled *Rocky Balboa* comes in a close second. Not because I've always thought Sylvester Stallone total eye candy, but because of **The Speech**.

Rocky wants his kid to understand the meaning of character. He wants him to know what it means to be a man. To not allow others to point a finger in his face telling him he's nothing. Or worse, to believe them. He wants him to understand he is responsible for himself. That blaming other people or circumstances or even a big shadow will never help him in life. Only cowards blame other things. Rocky emphasizes that life will literally beat you to the ground if you let it, hitting you harder than anything else ever could. Then comes the best part of his speech for me. He tells his son how to win. How winners are made. He explains that—all I can do at this point is quote him—"It ain't about how hard you're hit. It's about how hard you can get hit and keep moving forward."

Now I'm gonna get personal. Only because I must. Fathers must teach their son(s) this lesson. If not, we'll all end up having to deal with a bunch of marshmallows instead of men. Rocky lets his son know how much he loves him. But he warns him that he'll never have a life if he doesn't start making changes.

I came away saying, "Wow! Now that's a speech!" Check it out sometime.

Imagine if everyone thought like that. There's one good reason why they don't. It's just too stinkin' hard. It's easier to give up or blame someone or something else. It's easier when it's not my fault. Maybe we should just carry around a sign that reads, *It's Not My Fault!* Certainly Robert Balboa, Jr. felt that way. He couldn't help being born the only son of Rocky Balboa—the Heavy Weight Champion of the World. The fact that people wondered why he hadn't turned out like his father couldn't possibly be laid on him. That seemed to be the reason he couldn't get anywhere in life. So what, exactly, was this kid's fault? Anything? He just had the misfortune of standing in the shadow of Rocky Balboa.

One person never stood in the shadow of Rocky Balboa. Adrianna "Adrian" Pennino. Also known as Mrs. Rocky Balboa. Why not? How did Adrian avoid falling victim to Rocky's shadow? It's certainly not due to her flamboyant, sophisticated, or self-assured nature. She possessed none of those traits. She was shy, humble, insecure, but mostly decent. She surrounded herself with her brother, Paulie, and the lousy pet shop where she worked. If you passed her on the street, you would never notice her. Some might even call her homely. But Rocky saw in her something no one else saw: personal internal strength. Adrian didn't reveal this quality in a way that others would notice. Only Rocky saw it. So the one time he quit, he drew from Adrian's strength.

What about Mickey Goldmill, Rocky's trainer and

manager? At first glance, one wouldn't think of Mickey as the sort of fellow who stood in anyone's shadow. Talk about flamboyant! But Mickey had his own set of demons. An "I almost made it" boxer with a truckload of regrets, Mickey came with his own excuses. "I never had no trainin'" or "I ain't never had nobody to take an interest," were his words. I remember being taught you had to create your own interest. Mickey's need to give Rocky what he never received was really the opportunity to turn back the hands of time in an effort to lay down his mark. A mark he didn't make as a young fighter. He'd become a nobody. The shadows Mickey stood in were all the boxers who went on to be greats.

Rocky becomes his salvation. In return, Rocky gives him respect, adoration, a reputation as a great trainer, but more importantly love. The kind of love a son has for a father. In the end, Mickey takes Rocky to great heights, but the heights turn out to be false. The fall is hard. Mickey dies. Rocky is faced with standing in his own shadow—the shadow of Rocky Balboa.

Shadows are funny things. They've always amazed me. The word *shadow* has multiple meanings. It can be used as a noun or a verb or an adjective. It can also be described as a threat. Multiple shadows appear if there are multiple light sources. During certain times of the day, like at sunrise or at sunset, there's the likelihood that shadows will become quite long. Let's say that the sun is directly overhead. If that happens, then the shadow will disappear completely.

Well, well, well, how's that for a coincidence? Let's do an analogy. Take a winner, put a loser up next to him. Consequently, there's nowhere to run or nowhere to hide. Poor Paulie and Rocky, Jr. never had a chance. Had they'd risen above, they never would have stood in the shadow of Rocky Balboa. But that would have taken work, believing in themselves, moving forward even after the beat-down, getting back up, actually doing something, digging down into their souls, grabbing hold of that personal internal strength. If they did that then who would they have to blame except…..

Throughout all the *Rocky* movies, a couple of guys *never* stood in the shadow of Rocky Balboa. Who? Cuff and Link! They could have cared less about this legend known as Rocky Balboa. They were content with their lives. If stress arose, they had a safe place to tuck their heads. They cared about being fed. Oh, to have the self-confidence of Cuff and Link. Don't know them? Watch the movies.

Standing in the shadow of Rocky Balboa can be a terrible thing. Not trying to get out is worse. Rocky was a body puncher. He went for the body like nobody's business. Take away a fighter's air and the only place he can go is down. Joe Frazier is quoted as saying, "Destroy the body, and the head will die." My greatest fear is that potentially great people will become complacent. They'll stop trying. They'll start accepting. Soon they'll stop working and expect entitlements. Ultimately, they'll become comfortable standing in the shadows. They'll forget how to be great.

The Bible speaks of how God disciplines His sons in Hebrews 12:1-13. I'm struck by how it parallels with what Rocky wanted his son to grasp. Discipline and the building of one's character. It reads so beautifully: "Therefore, since we are surrounded by such a great cloud of witnesses, let us throw off everything that hinders and the sin that so easily entangles. And let us run with perseverance the race marked out for us, fixing our eyes on Jesus, the pioneer and perfecter of faith.

For the joy set before him he endured the cross, scorning its shame, and sat down at the right hand of the throne of God. Consider him who endured such opposition from sinners, so that you will not grow weary and lose heart. In your struggle against sin, you have not yet resisted to the point of shedding your blood. And have you completely forgotten this word of encouragement that addresses you as a father addresses his son? It says, 'My son, do not make light of the Lord's discipline, and do not lose heart when he rebukes you, because the Lord disciplines the one he loves, and he chastens everyone he accepts as his son.' Endure hardship as discipline; God is treating you as his children. For what children are not disciplined by their father? If you are not disciplined—and everyone undergoes discipline—then you are not legitimate, not true sons and daughters at all. Moreover, we have all had human fathers who disciplined us and we respected them for it. How much more should we submit to the Father of spirits and live! They disciplined us for a little while as they thought best; but God disciplines us for our good, in order that we may share in his holiness. No discipline seems pleasant at the time, but painful. Later on, however, it produces a harvest of righteousness and peace for those who have been trained by it. Therefore, strengthen your feeble arms and weak knees. 'Make level paths for your feet,' so that the lame may not be disabled, but rather healed."

When Stallone wrote the now famous (in my mind only) Rocky speech, I'm rather curious to know if he knew these verses or how well they spoke to what he wanted his character to convey. Not sure. These scriptures pretty much teach that living in a shadow never works.

When a boxer is in the ring face-to-face with his opponent,

he better not be standing in anyone's shadow because there *is* no backup. It's a one-on-one sport. He has to do the work himself. No complacency, no acceptance, no entitlement. Just getting hit hard and moving forward. Boxing greats like Rocky Marciano, Joe Louis, James J. Braddock, Muhammad Ali, Jack Dempsey, and Smokin' Joe Frazier, all had that personal internal strength that made them winners. Talk about casting some shadows. Well, I'm sure I never ever want to be caught standing in the shadow of Rocky Balboa!

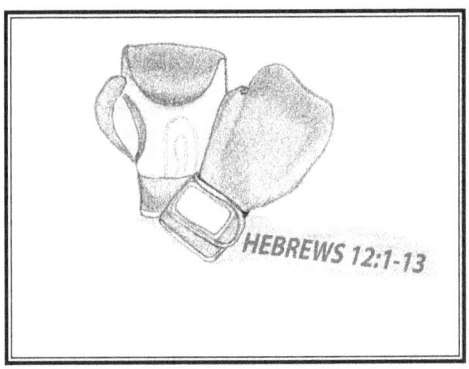

Chapter Fourteen

THE WAYS AND MEANS OF ATTICUS FINCH

*F*OR ME, MOVIES PIVOT ON A CHARACTER. TAKE FOR instance, *To Kill A Mockingbird, Gone With the Wind, Cat on a Hot Tin Roof, Long Hot Summer, Three Faces of Eve, A Streetcar Named Desire, Fried Green Tomatoes, Divine Secrets of the Ya-Ya Sisterhood, Steel Magnolias, The Green Mile, My Dog Skip.* Good stuff. My Southern roots are definitely showing. Southern or not, many folks would be willing to watch any of these movies more than once. I've watched a few of them a lot more than once or twice. I never tire of them.

My favorite, *Gone with the Wind*, premiered on December 15, 1939, in Atlanta, Georgia, at the Loew's Grand Theatre. The first public screening was, in fact, held at the glorious Fox Theatre to an unsuspecting audience. I know this because I lived in Atlanta a long time. In order to be a resident there you gotta know this stuff.

Even many years later, the Fox would periodically hold showings of *Gone with the Wind*. A dear friend and I would dress up in our gaudy best—high heels, all the rhinestones and fake pearls we could lay our hands on—and off we'd go to view this magnificent portrayal of turmoil throughout the South. We saw it every time the Fox ran it. It's a memory I hold close to my heart.

Like *Gone with the Wind*, each of the movies I mentioned previously contain a pivoting character that leaves you either wanting more or wanting to see them run off a cliff. But only one of these movies has a character so strong that I, for one, have always wished I knew someone like him. Or better yet, could step inside the story, live there, and call him my friend. *To Kill a Mockingbird* showcases such a character.

Released on December 25, 1962 *To Kill a Mockingbird* jumped off the screen like gangbusters. I was ten years old at the time. Controversy followed its debut. Due to the subject matter, my parents never would have allowed me to see it. But I actually *did* see it. I remember it vividly. I had a friend who lived down the street. Her mother, known to everyone as quite a character, knew no bounds to influencing her daughter's friends in whatever direction she saw fit. When the movie came out, she decided we should all see it, with no thought to what *my* parents thought.

The local drive-in theatre's marquee announced the movie in large block letters. Since my friend and I were only ten, she knew there would be no way she could get us into the drive-in, so she hid us in the trunk of her car and drove us all right into that drive-in completely undetected by the man at the ticket booth. After we parked at the microphone stand, she got us out of the trunk. We all sat on the hood of the car and watched the forbidden movie. Had my parents found out, I wouldn't be alive today to share this story—neither would my friend's mother. But it was worth the risk, making it the most exciting thing I'd ever experienced. At the ripe old age of ten, I became captivated by the characters projected onto the screen, brought to life out of the pages of Harper Lee's novel. I've carried that memory with me ever since.

Atticus Finch is an amazing character—a true Southern Gentleman, honorable, noble, decent. A widower, raising his two children, Jem and Scout, in a town in Alabama in the mid-1930s. A lawyer defending a black man accused of raping a white woman. Atticus treated all people with respect. It just came naturally to him. His education put him intellectually above the majority of those around him. However, he never made anyone feel as if he were better than they were.

He not only believed in the law, he lived by it, too. He

believed in the courts. Due process under the law. He believed in justice as well as equality. He found none of these things while defending his client. Because of his beliefs, he thought the twelve men in the jury box would see past race, look at the facts, and uphold the law. He was wrong. That didn't stop him from defending Tom Robinson. These were the ways and means of Atticus Finch.

What are *ways and means* anyway? There are multiple definitions. We should all remember from our government classes that in that context *ways and means* is the money that's available to meet what the government has budgeted to spend. It comes about through taxes or the raising of loans. We should also remember from our government class that there's a legal definition, as well, that talks about a committee that has jurisdiction over the country's ways and means. How's that for dipping into the old brain and pulling out stuff.

But I sometimes like to separate words like this because they make one look at them from a different slant. So, *means* is actually money, yes? Or maybe better said, one's property or personal wealth. Kinda like saying "he's a man of means." But then, *means* can also be a math term. I only know that because my daughter is a math teacher. I don't even know how to define it. She tried to explain it to me, but I just didn't get it. Never write about something you know nothing about. So I won't go there.

Now if you look at the word *way(s)*, we all know that it's how (or the way) we reply back to someone politely, or how we might lead the way with a plan. Legally it has a different meaning.

It occurred to me that *ways and means* simply put is: if you have the money, it's okay to spend it, as long as you don't

A PLACE CALLED *Common Sense*

go over the amount you set aside. Additionally the country is allowed to go about getting the money it needs, in order to take care of whatever the country needs. Where all the trouble begins is when we blow the budget, taking care of what the country wants, instead of what the country needs.

We all know, once again from government and/or history classes, what the Ways and Means Committee is, right? The initial version, established in 1789, only lasted eight weeks before it was dissolved and then in 1802 became a regular standing committee. Originally, it held the responsibility or the power over taxes and spending. In 1865, the spending power was turned over to a new bunch of guys who were called the Appropriations Committee. Now here's the scary part. Throughout history, the Chairman of the Ways and Means Committee has been one of the most powerful members of Congress. You can almost hear the theme song of *Jaws* (literally) in the background. Some pretty aggressive dudes have been running this show in the past.

So, what in the world does all of this have to do with Atticus Finch? Absolutely nothing, you say? Actually, there *is* a connection. Stick with me here. We really needed to go back and look at the short history of ways and means through government to understand that the ways and means of individual people is also a very serious thing. The *ways* in which we do things, and the *means* by which we attain those things are important. Which brings me to the question—what really were the ways and means of Atticus Finch?

Atticus Finch had a way of treating people that harbored no prejudice. The means by which he attained that attitude came through his character. Take, for instance, Mrs. Dubose. A crotchety old woman who hated everyone—particularly children. She sat on her porch snarling at the world. Then along came Atticus Finch. With a few words, he completely disarmed her. Keep in mind that he had just heard the old bag call his daughter an "ugly girl" after telling her not to say "hey" to her. She wanted Scout to be more respectful. She wanted her to say, "Good afternoon, Mrs. Dubose." Knowing my temper at Scout's age, I would have thrown a cow chip at her. Without missing a beat, Atticus stepped in, removed his hat and offered up the respect Mrs. Dubose demanded. He proceeded to tell her she looked like a picture. Then for the cream: He complimented her on her flower garden. He even compared them to the gardens at Bellingrath. He then tied it all up in a nice little bow by saying that her yard would be the showplace of the town. It was the ways and means of Atticus Finch.

Enter Tom Robinson, along with his wife and family, who were decent, hard-working people. Tom ended up in the wrong place at the wrong time. His naiveté put him there. Thinking he could help a white woman. Believing he could actually feel sorry for a white woman. The attraction of a white woman toward a black man. He never saw it coming. It just didn't happen. Or if it did, it wasn't to be talked about. It certainly better not be found out.

With the deck stacked against him, Tom faced his doom. All white jury. All men. All uneducated. All racists. As difficult as it was to admit to himself, Atticus knew it, but he never hesitated when asked to defend Tom Robinson. When he knew the facts, he knew Tom to be innocent. His defense of Tom Robinson could not have been better. Tom's innocence became obvious as the trial progressed. Atticus proved it over and over again. He never displayed anything other than respect when dealing with Tom or his family. It was the ways and means of Atticus Finch.

What about Mayella Violet Ewell? White trash? Most would agree. Where did a term like that come from anyway? Surprisingly, it originated in the Washington, DC, and Baltimore areas sometime around the 1820s. In the book, *A Key to Uncle Tom's Cabin*, which was written by Harriet Beecher Stowe, there's a chapter entitled "Poor White Trash." So, the term "white trash" or "poor white trash" is a term that's been used throughout literature, film, television, and music—all the way up to present day. Degrading? Certainly. But could any of us think of another person who deserved to be called poor white trash more than Miss Mayella? She was certainly poor. Certainly white. Definitely came across as trashy. Ignorant, illiterate, pathetic. Most men would have passed her by without a glance or thought.

Maybe a refresher course in The Ten Commandments might have been in order for Miss Mayella as Exodus 20:16 reads: "You shall not give false witness against your neighbor."

Throughout the cross-examination of Mayella Ewell, Atticus called her Miss Mayella. He certainly had the right to call her by her first name, as the Prosecutor did, but he didn't. He knew her to be a liar. He knew she was protecting herself at the expense of an innocent man. Still, he addressed her respectfully as Miss Mayella. It was the ways and means of Atticus Finch.

Then we see Robert E. Lee 'Bob' Ewell. Two words for this guy—racist pig. Or as my people, the Cherokee Indians, would say "Unega Gihli," which, when translated means, White Dog. Bob Ewell not only lied under oath, but I'm of the opinion that he beat and raped his own daughter. I also believe he beat her extra when he found out she had an attraction for a black man.

Atticus knew it. Bob Ewell not only lied on the witness stand, he lied to the sheriff to protect himself.

Proverbs 17:7 tells us: "Eloquent lips are unsuited to a godless fool—how much worse lying lips to a ruler!" As the reader of the novel and a viewer of the film, my belief has always been that the knowledge of Bob Ewell's abusiveness is the reason Atticus defended Tom Robinson in the first place, regardless of Tom's race. It became a matter of justice. For Atticus, simply right versus wrong—guilt versus innocence. Through it all, Atticus never showed any disrespect for Bob Ewell, proving himself a better person than I. It was the ways and means of Atticus Finch.

Along comes Arthur 'Boo' Radley. A tortured soul who knew no justice. His existence revolved around the scary house no one wanted to pass in front of. Some said he attempted to kill his family. Some said he spent his days locked up in the basement of the courthouse. Some said he almost died there. Some said he stabbed his father with a pair of scissors. Some said.... But he was just a man. A simple-minded man with no education, no social skills, no communication skills, no friends, no real life or future to mention. Until one night he became a hero. A rescuer of two kids who had nothing to do with the current events in their town. They only had the misfortune of being the offspring of Atticus Finch. The man who defended a black man.

Boo Radley saved two lives. Some might say, "Well, he took a life. That was wrong. He was nothing more than a vigilante. What do you expect from a crazy man?" Boo Radley was no crazier than Bob Ewell. Boo Radley never tried to kill a mockingbird. Boo Radley *was* the mockingbird, as was Tom Robinson. Ultimately, Boo Radley settles the score for the killing of the mockingbird.

Galatians 6:7–8 tells us: "Do not be deceived: God cannot

be mocked. A man reaps what he sows. Whoever sows to please their flesh, from the flesh will reap destruction; whoever sows to please the Spirit, from the Spirit will reap eternal life." I guess Bob Ewell learned that the hard way. When Scout spots Boo standing in the shadows behind the door, she calls out to him. Atticus, in his Southern Gentlemanly manner, says, "Miss Jean Louise, Mr. Arthur Radley." You would not have found one person in that town who would have shown that kind of respect to a man like Boo Radley. It was the ways and means of Atticus Finch.

Mockingbirds are known for their innate ability to mimic the songs of other songbirds. In fact, in only a few months, a mockingbird can actually master one hundred and eighty calls. Additionally, a mockingbird can also master over four hundred song types. Unfortunately for the mockingbird, his own tone is harsh. It has a bubbling sound to it, so it adapts itself to the sounds of others. Atticus told his children it was a sin to kill a mockingbird because all they do is sing. They never harm anyone or anything. Miss Maudie Atkinson told Jem, "There are some men in this world who are born to do our unpleasant jobs for us. Your father's one of them." Maybe Atticus was a mockingbird, too.

So how does one describe Atticus Finch? Jesus said it best in Matthew 5:43–48 as we read: "You have heard that it was said, 'Love your neighbor and hate your enemy.' But I tell you, love your enemies and pray for those who persecute you, that you may be children of your Father in heaven. He causes his sun to rise on the evil and the good, and sends rain on the righteous and the unrighteous. If you love those who love you, what reward will you get? Are not even the tax collectors doing that? And if you greet only your own people, what are you doing more than others? Do not even pagans do that? Be perfect, therefore, as your heavenly Father is perfect." When I think of the character Atticus Finch, I remember those words, because Atticus was that kind of man.

Now, let's drop Atticus Finch right into the middle of all this ways and means stuff. He was a man who had the ways of a great diplomat and the meager means of a country lawyer. Respect, honor, decency, patience, diplomacy, dignity, humor, intelligence. These are all words that describe a good man. A good Southern Gentleman. Atticus Finch was the cornerstone of his community. Atticus Finch had a strong affection for those around him. Atticus Finch stood for justice. He upheld the law. He loved his children. He wanted them to see the world as he saw it. He wanted them to grow into adults who would go on to be the cornerstones of their communities. He gave to everyone around him. I saw all this in the character of Atticus as I sat on the hood of my friend's mother's car. The forbidden movie that showed me how a character such as Atticus could rise above the discourse and shine a light on goodness even in the darkness of tragedy. It was the ways and means of Atticus Finch.

Chapter Fifteen

WHAT IN THE WORLD IS STONE SOUP?

*T*he first time I heard "The Story of Stone Soup" I heard it on one of my favorite television programs, *Little House on the Prairie*. Caroline Ingalls told this story to her daughter Laura's class. I thought it would be interesting to look up the story to see how it compared to Caroline's version. I soon discovered that there are several versions of "The Story of Stone Soup." I must admit, after reading several of them, I liked Caroline's the best. She tells the story from an American Revolution perspective, with a British soldier as the main character. Take a listen sometime to Caroline's. You'll like it.

One thing about this story that I find amazing is that The Great Depression brought its own version. Families were strapped for cash and so putting food on the table seemed impossible most days. This tale took a different slant during this time when families found it necessary to actually put a rock in the bottom of a stockpot. When food was available, the rock would absorb the flavor of the food; when they had no food, the rock would be boiled with gallons of water, and the flavors that the rock absorbed previously would then flavor the "soup."

I decided I would try my hand at writing my own version, taking my cue from Caroline along with others that I read. From that I came up with the following:

Pretend that you are a young British soldier. Now pretend you are hungry, cold, and lost. You are far from home, in unfamiliar surroundings. In fact, you are in a wild country to your way of thinking. No one wants you there. The people in this strange place won't even open their doors to you or offer you a morsel of food or a drop of water. How would you feel?

As this young man wanders out of the forest and stumbles into the small village, he is ever so weak. He is freezing. His name is Samuel. As he walks down the street of the village, he knocks on each door asking for food or simply a warm place to stay. He volunteers to do all sorts of chores to earn his keep. The people of the village either slam their door in his face or don't answer the door at all.

What do you think Samuel did? I can tell you he did not go back into that forest only to starve to death. Not Samuel. He went into the middle of town. Then he took off his knapsack. The next thing he did was to find a big black iron pot. He filled it with snow. After that he built a fire under the pot. He stoked the fire until it became roaring hot. The snow melted quickly after that. The water started to bubble.

Samuel noticed, out of the corner of his eye, that the people in the village were peeking out of their windows. They were wondering what in the world he was doing. Their curiosity grew when Samuel pulled three shiny round rocks out of his knapsack. He dropped each rock into the pot while the people watched. Then, when the water came to a rolling boil, he took a great big spoon out of his knapsack and began stirring the concoction.

After he stirred the water, he dipped out a spoonful so he could smell it. He had the biggest smile on his face. It was as if it were the best smelling food in the whole wide world. By this time, all the villagers had come out of their houses to see what Samuel was doing. They all stood around the steaming pot. Finally, a little girl asked Samuel what he was cooking. What do you think Samuel said? Stone Soup! But before anyone could ask any more questions, Samuel tasted the soup.

Then he said the soup would be much better if only it had some onions in it. An old man in the crowd said he just might have some onions. He left. When he came back, he had a bunch of onions in his hands. So Samuel put them into the pot then tasted the soup again. He looked around the crowd and said that if he only had some potatoes or carrots the soup would be even better. The people somehow found the potatoes *and* the carrots. They gave them all to Samuel. Obviously, they had been hiding food. With the addition of the potatoes and carrots, the soup began to smell delicious now.

Next, the people added some beef bones. Then Samuel said the soup was done. He decided to give the old man first taste because he contributed first. Can you guess what the old man said after he tasted the soup? He said it was the best stone soup he ever had! Just as though he had been eating stone soup his entire life.

Good story! At the end of the story there's a moral. Caroline left it up to each individual student to get from the story whatever they might. She offered no opinion of her own. She wanted the students to think for themselves.

I offer up a few suggestions for your consideration:

1. By working together, with everyone contributing whatever he or she can, a greater good is achieved.
2. When everyone shares, the overall flavor of the soup improves.
3. As we work together in cooperation with each other, we end up better off than when we started.
4. If there is something you want people to do, never tell them how much they are needed; create the illusion that

you are giving them the opportunity to be a part of the overall success of the project.
5. In the "Nail Soup" version, the moral is to be leery of strangers offering absolutely nothing in exchange for a small amount of something.

New traditions of "The Story of Stone Soup" are gaining in popularity. I've known people who gather their friends or family and a pot of stone soup is served. We're talking *real* stone soup with a *real* stone in it. This gathering happens every so often. Maybe once a month or so. After the soup is ladled into bowls, each person is served. The person whose bowl contains the stone, is then responsible for cooking the stone soup at the next gathering. Sounds like fun. Anything that brings family and friends together is always a good idea.

My husband and I have our kids over for dinner every Sunday. The laughter and fun we share is priceless. It's a time when we stop and just enjoy being a family. There's no stress, no time crunch, no worldly madness. We simply gather together. Kind of like the fellowship shared at a stone soup dinner. We look forward to Sunday dinners. I wouldn't trade our time together for anything in the world.

Looking at the different morals of "The Story of Stone Soup," I find it's actually all five of the morals I listed combined. The British soldier enticed the people by acting as though he'd just cooked up the most delicious soup ever to grace the table of any nobleman of any country on the planet. He made them so curious they could no longer stay closed up in their houses. They had to see what was going on with this guy. He taught them that through teamwork anything can be accomplished. More importantly, he made them feel a part of the success of satisfying the hunger they were all suffering from by contributing something they claimed they didn't have.

This is why people come together in tragedy. We as a people seem to be at our best when helping others who have suffered extreme hardships. Look at September 11th or Hurricane Katrina or the tsunamis that have hit in various places. Look at the homeless problem or the outbreak of AIDS in Africa. People love the act of helping. That's where egos can come into play, because it makes us all feel good to help. It strokes the ego a bit. We walk a fine line with that when we reach out to help. If we're honest with ourselves, we will admit that part of why we help is how it makes us feel. Ask anyone who's been a part of a mission group. They'll admit that they've received far more than they ever gave. It's a feel-good thing. I'm not purporting that it's wrong or that anyone feeling that way is a self-centered, egotistical schmuck. I'm just saying it is human nature.

"The Story of Stone Soup" truly is an uplifting story. It's a story of teamwork, of pulling together in an effort to help one another. When we hear any story, whether it's "The Story of Stone Soup," or any story with a moral, we must look at all sides. Dig into it to see if the author is trying to make more than one point. If we take what we can get from it, learn, debate, agree, or even disagree, we can walk away with some sort of consensus. Certainly, the most optimistic moral would be working together.

The Bible instructs us in the way in which we are to help each other, work together, or maybe even help those less fortunate. In the Book of 1 John 3:17 we read: "If anyone has material possessions and sees a brother or sister in need but has no pity on them, how can the love of God be in that person?

Dear children, let us not love with words or speech but with actions and in truth."

In Hebrews 13:16 we read: "And do not forget to do good and to share with others, for with such sacrifices God is pleased." Proverbs 29:7, also reads: "The righteous care about justice for the poor, but the wicked have no such concern." Then in Deuteronomy 15:7-8 we read: "If anyone is poor among your fellow Israelites in any of the towns of the land the Lord your God is giving you, do not be hardhearted or tightfisted toward them. Rather, be openhanded and freely lend them whatever they need."

My favorite as it pertains to helping one another, working together, or helping those less fortunate, is found in Matthew 25:35–40 as it reads:

"For I was hungry and you gave me something to eat, I was thirsty and you gave me something to drink, I was a stranger and you invited me in, I needed clothes and you clothed me, I was sick and you looked after me, I was in prison and you came to visit me.' Then the righteous will answer him, 'Lord, when did we see you hungry and feed you, or thirsty and give you something to drink? When did we see you a stranger and invite you in, or needing clothes and clothe you? When did we see you sick or in prison and go to visit you?' The King will reply, 'Truly I tell you, whatever you did for one of the least of these brothers and sisters of mine, you did for me.'"

Doing nothing is never an option. When we choose to do nothing, we accomplish nothing. "The Story of Stone Soup" teaches us how to do a thing collectively. Look at how God set up parts of the animal and insect worlds. Ants, bees, horses, giraffes, zebras, coyotes, and monkeys are all groups of animals and insects that work together.

"The Story of Stone Soup" fits right in with the Bible verses by showing how one lone British soldier brought together an entire village who didn't want to know him.

Stories are wonderful things. They make us feel good. They incite us. They make us think. They make us cry. They make us laugh. They teach us. They leave us with morals (the practical lessons of the story). Or maybe even morals (the principles or rules of right conduct).

For me, "The Story of Stone Soup" made me want to learn more, mainly because when I first heard the title, I thought… what in the world is stone soup? Now I know!

Chapter Sixteen

WHEN LEADERS EMERGE

My daddy told me once, "Gene, (he called me Gene) here's Leadership 101: take a piece of string. Now lay it on a table. With your finger try to push it. What happens? It becomes a backed-up mess. Now, straighten it out. With your thumb and index finger take hold of the string and pull it. What happens? It follows wherever you lead it." He also said, "Too many cooks in the kitchen spoils the dish." I tend to agree. I believe there only needs to be one boss, one leader, one person who calls the shots. One final decision maker.

Leadership comes in all genres. Presidents of countries-companies-universities, owners of small businesses, school principals, school teachers, military generals, parents. Here's where I believe things get messed up. Too many voices. Too many viewpoints.

Here's why I believe this. I used to work for an association. When I interviewed with this association, it was for their "Director of Meetings." I landed the interview due to my level of qualifications. During the course of the interview, I asked this question, "What is the limit of my power?" This is a very important question to ask because whether they tell you that you have unlimited power or whether they tell you that you have restrictive power, you then have the option of accepting or declining the position. Just hope they answer truthfully.

I made a huge mistake. Being an association, they had boards plus committees plus chairs, all wanting a voice. I never took that into consideration when applying. Need I say, too many cooks in the kitchen? Maybe it's just me, but if my name is going to be attached to something, if the buck stops with me when it comes to the success or failure of an event, I want to run the show. That's leadership. That's how leadership works.

What happens when leaders emerge? They actually dare to dance in the path of greatness. It takes bravery to lead, and fortune ultimately rewards the brave. Leadership is simply the ability to lead. The word *lead* is just a going before others showing them the way. Like the string. Bear in mind that it's also a way to serve.

I started thinking about the real leaders that I've learned about over the years. Wouldn't it be fun to make a list? Yeah, well, I'm a nerd, so making lists works for me. Hopefully you'll indulge me and won't zone out on this bit of history nerdiness. Being from a Native American background, I decided to make a list of the most-valued real Native American leaders I learned about growing up.

Tatanka Yotanka – Most know him as "Sitting Bull." Known as the main leader of the Lakota People (originally the Dakota; later part of the Sioux), Sitting Bull led the Battle of the Greasy Grass, also known as The Battle of the Little Bighorn—or my favorite, Custer's Last Stand.

Ma-ca-tai-me-she-kia-kiak – Most know him as "Black Hawk." He actively fought not only for his nation's lands but also for their sovereignty. He fought in the War of 1812 and the Blackhawk War.

Sequoyah – Created the Tsalagi alphabet which is also known as the Cherokee alphabet. A Tsalagi leader. The Tsalagi people were later known as the Cherokee. Not only a great warrior and leader, but also a great thinker.

Tecumseh – Leader of the Shawnee. Tecumseh spent most of his life in defense of his nation's lands.

Crazy Horse – Best known for his participation and leadership in the Battle of the Little Bighorn, he was a leader of the Oglala Lakota people and considered a good warrior.

Cochise – Well-known Apache Chief who was initially quite friendly with the white man. Unfortunately, the U.S. army hanged some of Cochise's relatives. At that point, Cochise waged war on the army, becoming relentless in his endeavor. Known for his military skills, his integrity, and his courage.

Geronimo – Known as the leader of a Chiricahua group and part of the Apaches, he was captured and escaped several times. He ended up as a very prosperous farmer after becoming a Christian.

Although there are many great Native American leaders, those listed are, in my opinion, among the best. Over the years, lists of great leaders have been published. Some I thought were excellent. Some—not so much.

Abraham Lincoln comes to mind as a great leader. Mainly because Lincoln successfully led the country through the American Civil War, also known as the War Between the States. Lincoln's victory not only ended slavery but also preserved the Union. Oddly enough, Lincoln got his share of vilification. Many hated him, most likely because he made difficult decisions that weren't popular but turned out to be the right ones.

Another great leader might have been Alexander the Great, known as the greatest most successful military commander of all time. According to legend, Alexander the Great went undefeated in battle. Born in 356 BC, he died 323 BC from either malaria or poisoning, one month short of his thirty-third birthday. He reigned from 336-323 BC, or thirteen years. It's believed that he might have suffered from congenital scoliotic disorder, which is a spinal and neck deformity.

Leaders come in all shapes and sizes. Some are radicals or fanatics, even zealots. I guess it's all in how one defines the word "leader." Even the most evil amongst us lead. In my naïve mind, I consider leadership a noble thing. A leader is a person we look up to with admiration. Someone who makes us feel safe because we know that person is capable of leading the way. Leaders must be strong in character, sharp in mind. If not, then how could they possibly lead?

Turning our attention to fictitious leaders, my all-time favorite is Maximus Decimus Meridius from the movie *Gladiator*. I love him. Another is King Leonidas from the film *300*. How about Captain John H. Miller from *Saving Private Ryan*? Who could forget Captain James Kirk from the all-time favorite television program and movie *Star Trek*? All fictitious leaders, but leaders just the same.

In those times when leadership is needed, it's often difficult to find that person who qualifies. A couple of things come into play. When the prospect of a leader appears, we don't always recognize it. If by chance we do, it suddenly becomes difficult for that leader to lead. Why? The grabbing at political power that morphs into political greed might be one reason. I guess it's back to too many cooks in the kitchen. We see few who are willing to dance in the path of greatness. I'm thinking many lost their nerve. Leadership requires one to not only have nerves of steel, but also exceptional judgment. The two go hand-in-hand. Exceptional judgment allows a leader to make hard or, if necessary, fast decisions. Too many of those in charge don't have that ability. A true leader must stand for something.

Doing hard things well is difficult. We live in a country founded by men who knew how to do many hard things well. My biggest fear is that our children will never know how to do that. We spend our time defending, rewarding, or making excuses for bad behavior. Far too many times we cave under pressure.

Extreme circumstances sometimes can bring forth strong leadership. The question then becomes whether or not that strong leadership will continue or whether it's just a temporary thing. After September 11th, some said the President emerged as a strong leader. In the weeks following September 11th, that approval rate topped at ninety-two percent. It went progressively downhill after that, spiking only a few times. Fast forward a couple of years and the temperament of the people took another turn. So what changed? Probably the fact that we live in an instantaneous world that wants what it wants when it wants it. Meaning right now. The problem with that point-of-view is that hard things take time. So how long must we wait? How long is a long time?

Leadership is difficult in that when leaders make hard decisions people demand instantaneous results. We want our leaders to fix any given issue or situation now. We don't want to wait. Our impatience causes bad results, whether it's the economy, the war on terror, immigration, world relations, healthcare, or even fame.

Leadership actually pivots on the leader's ability to lead. Our country, our churches, our corporations, our schools, all need leaders who actually have the ability to lead. Without that ability, well…

True leaders lead even when those who are being led don't know it. Now that's a gifted leader. True leaders motivate those they lead. Let us not confuse that statement with the "gah-gah effect" or even effective speaking. Just because one is an eloquent speaker doesn't mean one is cut out to be a leader.

Once upon a time I worked for a guy who I'd call a true leader. He did everything a leader is called to do. I know I would have gone to the mat for him. There were many times he had to make hard decisions that others in the company thought erroneous. He never backed down. Never caved to company pressure. In the end, he came out the victor. I admired him tremendously.

Looking at what the Bible says about leadership, Proverbs 28:2–3 tells us the following: "When a country is rebellious, it has many rulers, but a ruler with discernment and knowledge maintains order. A ruler who oppresses the poor is like a driving rain that leaves no crops. Those who forsake instruction praise the wicked, but those who heed it resist them."

Also in Proverbs 20:26: "A wise king winnows out the wicked; he drives the threshing wheel over them." Romans 13:3 speaks clearly to leaders as well. Leadership in these passages is clear, but nothing says it like Matthew 20:25–28 as we read: "Jesus called them together and said, 'You know that the rulers of the Gentiles lord it over them, and their high officials exercise authority over them. Not so with you. Instead, whoever wants to become great among you must be your servant, and whoever wants to be first must be your slave–just as the Son of Man did not come to be served, but to serve, and to give his life as a ransom for many;'" What's more, 1 Peter 5:1–4 reinforces it. What a great charge to leaders. To be servants. To be eager to serve. That's where the definition of a leader is lost on many who call themselves our leaders. They've lost sight of the fact that they are there to serve.

Jesus was and is the greatest leader of all time. Mark

10:45 puts leadership and the responsibility of leaders into perspective as it reads: "For even the Son of Man did not come to be served, but to serve, and to give his life as a ransom for many."

Great leaders are defined by the success of those they lead. Jesus led his disciples. Then He left them with the tools they needed to succeed. He understood that leaders don't just lead, they serve. They give their lives for those who follow them. Now I get that the world sees Jesus and his disciples as a group of men who were unsuccessful since they were ultimately killed. I disagree with that theory. There's certainly the possibility that could happen. It doesn't, however, negate the successfulness of that leader. Might I be so bold as to mention that the majority of the people think of Abraham Lincoln as a successful leader?

Remember Captain Richard Phillips, the American ship captain, who was held captive by the Somali pirates? Many called him a hero. I called him a great leader. He put up his life for the lives of his crew. Great leaders do that without pause. They are there to serve. Just like Jesus.

Today, far too many leaders, as they like to be called, bask in the glow of their own self-greatness. They have no idea how to make hard decisions because they are too busy admiring themselves, patting themselves on the back for what they believe is a job well done. Yet they sit and do nothing. Jesus gave His life so all of us could live. He suffered. He sacrificed. He served. He also dared to dance in the path of greatness simply because He represented the true definition of greatness itself. His bravery defies description.

Things happen in this life that make us wonder where this world is going. Sometimes those events are downright scary. Over the last few years, I find I've been shaken to my core. I would like to think that whatever the future holds for us all, we will at some point be able to recognize the exact moment when true leaders emerge.

Chapter Seventeen

WHEN SENSE AND SENSIBILITY LEFT THE BUILDING

A PLACE CALLED *Common Sense*

I've wondered recently, when it happened. When did sense and sensibility leave the building? Then it occurred to me. It left the building the day honest men walked out and greedy men walked in. It left when we all forgot how to work hard to earn an honest living.

Hard work is one of those terms that has somehow taken flight. It means nothing these days because hard work means one actually has to work. In order to accomplish anything, we have to work hard. I asked my granddaughter via text (amazing) how school was going. My granddaughter, fourteen years old at the time, a freshman in high school (also amazing), responded, "It's hard." I could tell by the sound of her texting that she didn't mean "it's hard" in a good way; she meant it's hard in an "I don't want to do it because it's hard" way. She knew that I knew because I could hear her in the background saying to herself, "Here comes a lecture." Yes, grandmothers can actually hear through phone texts, so remember that the next time you are texting your grandmother.

At this point, I felt lecture time had indeed arrived. I told her that even though it's hard she must keep working (she wants to be a doctor), because there's nothing in this life that's worth anything if you don't have to work for it. OMG! (Contrary to popular belief, OMG actually means O̲h M̲y G̲randmother.)

Suddenly, one of those reality talent shows flashed through my mind. You know, that instant fame thing. Admittedly, I enjoy viewing the talent. To be honest, the bad talent gives me a bit of a chuckle. But I've always had a problem with instant fame. That's not to say that there aren't those who try out for these shows who have not paid a bit of dues. But really, how many dues could they possibly have paid if the cut-off age is twenty-nine? I'm convinced that many young people really don't get the concept of "paying dues."

So I've asked myself repeatedly, did sense and sensibility leave the building when we stopped working hard? When we stopped being a nation of people who commit themselves to a worthwhile goal? When we stopped having pride in what we do? When we stopped respecting our country or our flag? When we looked for the street known as Easy? When we now take comfort in pushing that easy button? When we replaced consequence with acceptance? When we took shame out of everything? When we turned toward ourselves and turned away from God?

I can remember when I was a kid—those words set on fire the heads of every kid in the world. I know when I would say those words, my kids would run as fast as they could away from me, their eyes rolling in the back of their head, screaming all the way. I must admit that it always drove me crazy when my parents said those words, too, but they knew what they were talking about when they prefaced statements using those words. Getting back to *when I was a kid*, everything seemed different. When you got sent to the principal's office, it meant you were going to get paddled. Yes! Paddled! The on-your-butt paddled. Oh, the child abuse of it all. The absolute politically incorrectness! Don't tell anyone, but it worked.

Shame is a politically incorrect word. Most likely because it's defined as being a painful feeling. If you actually look up its definition, you'll certainly understand why the word has dropped out of our vocabulary.

I can remember when I was a kid (Hah! Oh yeah I did.)

there wasn't a single teacher in my school, first grade all the way through twelfth grade, who didn't know the meaning of shame. Or who wasn't afraid to use it on a daily basis. As my oldest daughter once said when she asked my husband whether or not baby Jesus was actually born in a stable, "Let's ask Mom; I bet she was there when baby Jesus was born." That should tell you when I was in school. So, naturally, *shame* has disappeared right along with sense and sensibility. They both left the building long ago.

What happened to all the honest men? What made them leave the building? Did they lose sight of things like honesty, hard work, commitment, giving one's word, and decency? I've not seen them lately. Not in the corporate world, certainly not in the political world. Much to my dismay, not even in the Christian world.

So where might one actually go to get a glimpse of an honest man since they seem to have left the building? For me, I turn my eyes toward the heavens. Then God taps me on the shoulder and says, "Being a little cynical are we? Did I not teach you to count your blessings? Take a look around." Okay, okay so I'm looking. Then my husband walks into the room. God smiles. I smile. "Well, that's only one good guy," I say. Then, God, in His special way, starts a slide show in my mind. I see the likes of my daddy, my grandfather, my uncles, and all the other men in my family. Then the show just keeps going. Then God says, "See, I told you."

Now that I know where all the honest men are, I realize why things are the way they are at this particular moment in time. My mind suddenly reflects back. I recall the words of that great philosopher, Clark W. Griswold, who said, "Take a look around you, Ellen, we're at the threshold of hell!" Let's face it. Times are pretty divisive. Multiple things are in play with no answers from what I have been able to discern. I fear it's because all those honest men—those honorable men that God so lovingly showed me—aren't the ones in power.

I can remember when I was a kid (Ha! I promise this is the last time.) my parents never gave me an allowance. They had a reason. Of course, at the time, I thought myself to be the product of child abuse. We weren't poor. My parents didn't have twelve other kids to give allowances to. They just had me. Never mind the fact that I had a room of my own, multiple outfits hanging in my closet, plenty of food and snacks to eat, toys, and shoes on my feet that actually fit. They never gave me an allowance because my parents didn't believe in giving children money to do the things they were supposed to be doing in the first place. They taught me that awards or rewards are not given for doing what you're expected to do. They're given for doing extraordinary things, for going over and beyond the call of duty. I had chores. I had to do my best in school. I had to be respectful to adults. I had to say, "Yes, sir" or "No, sir." "Yes, ma'am" or "No, ma'am." "Please" and "Thank you." In return, they allowed me to live.

Fast forward to today. I have a Merriam-Webster Dictionary (paperback), printed in 1989, which is probably when I bought it. It cost $4.95. I have no idea how many words are in it, but I know it has a lot. I decided to look up the word "bailout" in my 1989 dictionary. Guess what I found? It's not in there.

Then I decided to look it up on the Internet dictionary website. It's in there. I laughed out loud at some of its meanings.

In October of 2008 we saw a number of bailouts. Only

they didn't call it a bailout. They called it a rescue plan. They even passed a law for it. Those companies who benefited from it, I'd venture to say, were all led by those greedy men who walked into the building when the honest men walked out. Through all of this, I still ask the question, why? Why did the honest men walk out in the first place? I wish I knew. Is greed that powerful that it takes an honest man, gives him power, gives him money, then suddenly he becomes greedy? Maybe.

The Book of Hosea states in Chapter 13 verses 4–6: "But I have been the Lord your God ever since you came out of Egypt. You shall acknowledge no God but me, no Savior except me. I cared for you in the wilderness, in the land of burning heat. When I fed them, they were satisfied; when they were satisfied, they became proud; then they forgot me." Therein lies the rub.

Years ago I took on the responsibility of directing a play for my Sunday school class. During the Christmas season, we would always gather at the Church to have a class Christmas party. We loved it, because we came together to celebrate the birth of Christ, as well as to share the joys of the holiday with the fellowship of good friends. Plus there was always the food! Each year we would have a talent show or a play or some sort of entertainment.

This one particular year I lost my mind and volunteered to direct a play. The play entailed a fashion show featuring men and women's attire that, when described by the fashion show host on stage, was literally what they were wearing. For instance, if the host described an A-Line dress or skirt, which of course is a dress or skirt shaped like the letter "A," then the outfit would actually look like the letter "A." A bubble skirt would actually be bubbles; a fishtail skirt would be a fishtail; spaghetti strap…well, you get it. On paper it sounds rather boring, but in person it's a scream.

It's vitally important to use your imagination while designing your costume. Having seen this play in the past, I found it never failed to delight the audience. I decided that instead of asking the members of my class to participate, I would invite the Drama Club at my oldest daughter's high school to put on the show for my Sunday school class. Upon announcing to my class my intentions, a voice came up out of the back of the room saying, "You must be out of your mind!" Well, that seemed an idiotic thing to say. I already knew that bit of info. No one drafted me. I took it on myself. Being out of my mind became a moot point. I ignored the voice then proceeded with my announcement.

One of the guys in my class just happened to be the Vice-Principal of my daughter's high school. I'd always thought him to be a rather nice sort. Always met you with a smile or how-do-you-do. We'd known each other for a few years. He even came to my house for a birthday party for my daddy.

Imagine my surprise when he pulled me aside and said, "Regina, I know you want this play to be a success, but some of the kids in the drama club are a bit on the unruly side. They never disappoint in how they behave. They are the kind of kids who you know are going to get into trouble, and that's exactly what they do. You might want to reconsider using this group."

Well, now. That sounded like a challenge to me. Politely thanked him for his concern, told him not to worry. I could handle it. Clearly I *was* out of my mind. This guy knew what he was talking about. He dealt with these kids on a daily basis. One of the things he said kept running through my mind: "They are the kind of kids who you know are going to get into trouble, and that's exactly what they do." Not on my watch, they wouldn't. And they didn't. The play went off without a hitch. My Sunday school class friends were laughing so hard they had tears running down their faces. I could not have been prouder of such an *unruly* bunch of kids in my life.

How does this story fit into the title of this chapter? It's quite simple. Hard work, commitment to a worthwhile goal, taking pride in what they did, not pushing the easy button, knowing that I *expected* them to do the work or they would suffer the consequences if they didn't. Knowing that I never shied away from using shame. More importantly, they knew they were in God's house. *He* expected them to be respectful. So they were. No greed involved. These kids got nothing out of this other than to have a group of adults, not to mention their own Vice-Principal, applauding their performance. Offering up a "Bravo! Job well done." Sense and sensibility were definitely in that room and on that stage that night.

It's funny, I can remember when I was a kid…yeah, I know. I said it was the last time. Well, I lied! As the only child of my parents, the very fact that they never gave me an allowance, expected me to do the right things, made me feel the consequences of my actions, or weren't afraid to use shame; it's funny, but I don't ever remember their having to bail me out of anything. I learned to do that on my own.

The realization is this, whether you listen to the news on TV or read about it in the newspapers or on the Internet, no matter how you get your information, we are what we are and we are where we are because we've lost the definitions of important words. We replaced them with words like "bailout" which, by the way, was Merriam-Webster's 2008 Word of the Year. That, my friend, is when sense and sensibility left the building.

Chapter Eighteen

WILL THE REAL TOWANDA PLEASE STAND UP?

REGINA STONE MATTHEWS

*T*HERE'S A TOWANDA LIVING IN THE SOUL OF EVERY woman. Whether or not Towanda ever emerges isn't the issue. She's there, either right beneath the surface or buried deep below. We have all known a few outspoken Towandas in our lives. Be they personally or throughout history. You may or may not know Towanda. She was the battle cry of one Idgie Threadgoode, a flamboyant character in the movie and novel *Fried Green Tomatoes*, written by Fannie Flagg. In the movie, Ninny Threadgoode is played by Jessica Tandy. Ninny possessed some Towanda in her. From what I saw of Jessica Tandy over the years, I always believed she had a bit of the Towanda inside of her as well.

Idgie Threadgoode, a tomboy, a bee charmer, a pain in the backside, a sinful creature, and a Towanda, never ceased to amaze me. In fact, it's my belief that Idgie used the word "Towanda" as her own battle cry whenever she did something daring, calling upon it whenever she needed that extra boost of courage during those times of doing what she shouldn't.

Ninny's friend, Evelyn Couch, soon learned from Ninny the power of Towanda. Ask any woman who has seen the movie. She'll tell you the best part of the movie comes when Evelyn bashes the ever-loving crud out of the car that stole her parking place. Two young little whippersnappers, known to every woman over the age of fifty as wenches, drove that car. I found myself right there with Evelyn. Screaming at the screen. Cheering her on. Saying things like—well, we won't go there. Let us just say Towanda came to Evelyn's rescue and did her proud. By the end of the scene, I had tears running down my face from laughing and screaming. I loved every minute of it. Probably because I knew I would never have the guts to do it. It's my bet that most others wouldn't either.

I'm proud of a few Towanda moments I've had in my life. Take the time this jerky little boy in third grade squeezed my hand so tightly it almost turned blue. Our school did this Maypole Dance at the local high school football field. If this tradition isn't familiar, simply put, it's a celebration of May Day, which is May 1st, or midsummer, where you partner up, hold hands, and dance around the maypole. Every kid hated it. Mainly because we were paired up with the opposite sex. When one is in the third grade, hating the opposite sex is a given. I had the misfortune of being paired up with this jerky kid who made my life miserable on a daily basis. I've often wondered whatever happened to him. I shudder to think. Probably doing time in some federal pen.

As the Maypole Dance started, this schmuck decided he'd see just how hard he could squeeze my hand. By the way, I had recently had surgery on my hand, which he knew about. That was the point. He knew he could hurt me. As the music to the Maypole Dance began, he started squeezing my hand. We both knew that I could do nothing. We were out in the middle of the football field with twenty million parents, teachers, and officials looking on. I had to grin and bear it.

When the dance was over…drum roll please…Towanda! There stood the kid bragging to all his guy friends about what a big deal he was. I walked up to him, tapped him on the shoulder, then proceeded to kick him right in the, well, you know. Towanda! So great!

I decided it would be interesting to check out some of the famous Towanda women of the world. I came up with a pretty impressive list. From the likes of Cleopatra to Joan of Arc to Pocahontas to Deborah Sampson to Sacagawea to Florence Nightingale to Harriet Tubman to Rosa Parks. All Towandas in their own right.

Then I turned to the Bible. Talk about extraordinary women. Towanda doesn't even begin to describe these women. They lived in a time when women didn't even count for anything other than providing men with their needs or giving birth. Certainly some men in Bible times respected, cherished, or even adored women. Nonetheless, being a woman put you very far down on the food chain. Because of the time, the accomplishments of these women made them even more extraordinary. Beginning with Mary (the Mother of Jesus) to Elisabeth (the mother of John the Baptist) to Esther to Anna to Eve to Deborah to Dorcas to Mary Magdalene to Rahab. There are more, but the list is too long to cover here.

It goes without saying that all of these women, whether they lived in Bible times or modern times, accomplished things that shaped the world. Should even just one of them not existed or not called on her inner Towanda to accomplish what she needed to accomplish, the world would have felt the loss.

I do chuckle when I think of the Towandas in my life. Looking back over the times when my girls were little, I can see Towanda in each of them. Starting with my oldest. This kid would rather climb trees than do anything. Once, while climbing a tree in the back yard of my parents' mountain home, she lost her footing and slid right down that tree. Face and all. By the time she got to the bottom of the tree, she'd become a total-body scab. That was only the beginning of her Towanda years. A tomboy at heart, just like her mother. Throughout her growing up years, she yelled Towanda more times than I care to recount.

Up next, my middle daughter. She decided to do the tree-climbing event as well. Same tree. Same body scab. Her escapades were little things, such as running the riding lawn mower into the air conditioning units, falling down a mountain, pretending to be Mary Lou Retton by doing flips on the monkey bars at school. Oh, the list goes on. All the while yelling Towanda at the top of her lungs.

Then my youngest daughter. She portrayed more of a princess Towanda. Pink and purple were her signature colors. Lace and satin were her fabrics of choice. No dirt ever came in contact with her body. She wore bows in her hair. She took hours to pick out her clothes. She held the title of the high maintenance Towanda.

As for me, the Towanda inside of me knew no bounds growing up. Probably because I took after the one who raised me. I could out run, out climb, out jump, out fight any guy in the neighborhood. Towanda was tattooed on my chest.

As luck would have it, I have met a few Towandas who taught me the lessons in life that are the most important. Those are the Towandas you want to pattern your life after. I knew Mrs. Ray as one of those Towandas. She entered our lives when my girls were growing up and instantly became a friend of our family. She touched our hearts in a way beyond words. A gift from God to all who knew her. Not famous, but a true Towanda. Her faith, her obedience to

God, her values, her morals were all the things one would hope to acquire throughout one's life.

When I think of her, I reflect back on Proverbs 31:10-31 that speaks to virtuous women and their wisdom. It's so worth the read as it brings forth extraordinary words that describe extraordinary women. All those women who have a bit of the Towanda living inside them. Women who know just when and how to bring Towanda to the surface. When they do, all I can say is look out!

When we allow our minds to drift back over the Towandas in our life, we would be wise to remember the lessons they've taught us. Idgie Threadgoode taught Ruth Jamison, taught Sipsey, taught Ninny Threadgoode, who taught Evelyn Couch the power of Towanda. A friend of mine used to say, "Know why women all go to the bathroom together? It's a plot to take over the world." Yep, I buy into that.

Although throughout history women have had to fight for every step forward, they still hold the key. That's the amazing part. Publicly, women have always struggled for equality. You know the equal pay for equal work thing. But here's the inconsistency. Women hold all the cards. That's why Towanda is alive and well, living quietly in the heart of every woman.

My list of amazing women revealed to me that women are special. Try making your own list. See who you come up with and how they have shaped your thoughts. We are complex creatures who fight amongst ourselves, scratch and claw, but come together as sisters and friends who love each other. All the while knowing we'd scratch the eyes out of any man who might do us harm. I know that when

I delve into the lives of all the famous women throughout history or remember all the courageously feisty women I've known in my own life, I try to locate that power of Towanda within them. I wonder which one deserves the prize. As I'm lost in thought, I can almost hear a voice in the distance saying, "Will the real Towanda please stand up?"

Chapter Nineteen

WHERE HAVE YOU BEEN ALL MY LIFE MICHAEL BUBLE?

A PLACE CALLED *Common Sense*

Throughout our marriage, my husband has always known that a few men out there would only have to say, "Would you," and I'd be history! Not really. I'm absolutely joking. I've always felt, however, that if my husband simply *thought* I might leave him for another man, then that might be a good thing. Keep them on their toes I always say.

I must confess in the early part of our marriage, I became totally infatuated with Sylvester Stallone. "What a hunk!" I'd exclaim. But, then, my husband is a hunk too. So that never worked. He knew he had me at hello, to coin a phrase. Let's face it, the man doesn't have a jealous bone in his body. Believe me, I tried. My husband just laughs. He does that to get my goat. So I threw poor Sylvester under the bus. Until Michael Buble! His voice is incredible. He ain't too shabby in the looks department, either. But it's his songs that affect me most.

As a young girl, I, along with every other young person, went bonkers when it came to celebrities. The very thought of meeting a celebrity spun my hormones out of control. As I've gotten older, and our culture has gotten older, the "celebrity" has taken on a whole new slant. One would really have to know me to understand that celebrity status no longer impresses me. The word in itself is defined as fame or renowned, or being celebrated. I find it difficult, at best, to apply that to a human being.

Sadly, I wonder how we arrived at this place where we honor celebrities more than we honor God. We celebrate the lives of celebrities more than our own lives. We acclaim the names of these people more than the name of Jesus Christ. As I step down off my soapbox, I recall Bob Dylan's song, "The Times They Are A Changing." Except I don't think he had any idea just how much times were going to change.

Certainly, I have no objections to the idea of celebrities. I admire their talent. Well, some of them. My objection is the pedestal that we, as lowly mortals, put them on. My daddy always told me that the higher up you place humans, the farther they have to fall. There's a part of Psalm 16:4 that reads: "Those who run after other gods will suffer more and more." Then there's Judges 10:14: "Go and cry out to the gods you have chosen. Let them save you when you are in trouble!" Finally, in Romans 1:22 we read: "Although they claimed to be wise, they became fools" I certainly can relate to that. I've been known to be a fool more times than I care to admit.

Why do we do it? Why do we prop these people up in such a way? Perhaps we're so unhappy in our own lives we have to look at someone else's life and covet theirs. Does this validate our own existence in some way? I've chosen not to do this. Not because I think I'm special, but because I've grown to learn that's not where my salvation lies.

Now I look at people's talent. In some, it's truly amazing. The writers, the singers, the actors, the artists. Their abilities are the things I admire. With that in mind, I must say, "So where *have* you been all my life, Michael Buble?

The first song I ever heard him sing was "Home." Wow. I love it, I love it, I love it! The words, his voice, everything. I decided to check out the lyrics. Reading each word gives me a bit of a different feel. I discovered that the lyrics were phenomenal. Check it out. You'll agree.

Within this song is the story of a guy who has achieved his dream. What he considered his mission in life. Most people live their entire lives never achieving their dream or even finding their mission in life. This guy does. Yet now all he wants to do is go home. Is he out of his mind? I know how far away I am from *my* dream. So the first time I heard this song I'm thinking, what a schmuck. He's traveling to countries and cities I only dream of seeing. He has the clamoring adoration of millions. So what's this guy's problem? As usual, when I think stupid things, God taps me on the shoulder and says, "You know better than that." I *do* know better than that.

He's not a schmuck at all. In fact, he's smarter and braver than most. He went, he saw, he experienced his dream. He took a trip to LaLa Land. When he came back down to earth, he realized what was important. He's not a lucky guy because he's achieved his dream. He's a lucky guy because he's achieved his goal then discovered his most important blessing. He realized that it's not just the dream, it's who you share the dream with that's most important. Even though a line of the lyrics might seem to sway away from this fact, it's clear that a dream means nothing if, when you accomplish it, there's no one there to share in the joy. That's why the guy has a yearning to go home. In the end, he takes his run at fame and dreams, then heads for the most important thing in his life.

Let's not get the wrong impression that I'm advocating sitting on one's behind or not achieving whatever one wants to achieve. What I *am* advocating is going after whatever your dream is but never losing sight of what's important. Dreams are great. Aspirations are great. Accomplishments are great. Human beings are better. Our life here on earth is no accident. There are reasons for our existence. God put us all together to share in each other's dreams. It makes the dream all that much sweeter.

Once Michael Buble had blown me away with "Home," I'm thinking it couldn't get any better. Wrong. It got better. One day I'm driving in my car, and I hear "Lost" by Michael Buble. Here we have a story about two people in love who somehow, over time, have lost sight of each other. When I heard this song for the first time, I thought, "Oh what a beautifully sad love song." Then I heard it again. I thought, "Is the guy a jerk?" Then I heard it yet again. I thought, "Oh he's not a jerk. He really loves her. They just got lost from one another for a little while." Yes? No? What say you?

Then I decided I needed to not only read the words, I needed to savor them. As usual, I came away with a completely different view. I know, I, for one, get caught up in the singer, the music, and the swaying. I mean come on. Michael Buble. Are you kidding? So I had to tear myself away from Michael in order to understand the meaning of the lyrics. Let me preface that by making the point that I am only looking at these lyrics from my perspective and what I see in them. I'm sure the writers had their own meaning, but for me, this is how I saw it when I read the lyrics.

As I read through the song, I was taken aback by how they are parallel to what we've seen our country experience over the past decade or so. The first six lines of the song are so right in line with what has happened to "we the people of the United States of America." As the song speaks of the couple not being able to believe it's over, it brought to mind the end of our country's innocence, the day of September 11th. The song speaks to watching the whole thing fall and never seeing the tragedy coming because people refuse to see what's in front of them.

For decades we, as a country, slept while madmen plotted our demise. How unfortunate that we learned the hard lesson that there just might be some truth in good things not lasting. As I read on, it got even eerier. Since that terrible morning of September 11th, the seasons have changed. We've cried buckets for what used to be. For the loss of lives since that day. We've come upon the realization that we're becoming a nation that would be unrecognizable to our Founding Fathers.

Next comes the part in the lyrics that expresses the essence of how life can turn. It speaks of how hard life can be. How it can drive us insane and also rip our souls right out of our bodies. I've always seen America at its best when faced with tragedy. As the song goes on to say, even though it seems that things around us have changed, we know that there is always one thing that will never change. The song speaks of the couple's love. It reminds them of the fact they will always be in each other's heart. I believe most of us hold this country dear. That's the one thing that brings us together in times of sorrow or change.

Finally, the words that bring comfort. You are not alone. How many times did Jesus say that? How many times do we read it in the Bible? It's amazing how hearing those words gives us strength. The song goes on to reassure the estranged love that the speaker is there for them. That they can still be together, holding on to each other until the trying time is over. Even when everything seems to be falling down around them, even when they can barely crawl out from under the garbage, they still hold on to one another. He finally reminds his love that they are not lost, because they know where their hearts lie. Just as "we the people of the United States of America" know where our hearts lie.

Granted, I've put a bit of a spin on the lyrics to show how they can fit, but fit they do. As I read through the lyrics, I see a country torn apart by whatever label one wants to attach to it. At this moment, we are definitely a country divided. In fact, I see among us an array of people who appear lost. The "you are not alone" part, for me, is God, who is always there for us. Some just choose to look the other way.

Time has a way of slipping past, as the song says. We get caught up or lost in the idols. We follow the stars, until we see only stars. We overlook the writing on the wall. It's a pity to watch something great become something so small. To see how we allow life to tear our souls apart.

In all the change, in all the craziness, this country still remains in *my* heart. If darkness wins, we will be lost forever. I choose not to look the other way. I choose not to be alone. I choose not to crawl. I choose not to be lost. I choose to listen when God says, "You are not alone. I am always there with you." Jesus said it best in that part of Matthew 28:20 as we read: "And surely I am with you always, to the very end of the age."

As I look back over the idols of my youth, all the heartthrobs who have come and gone, I focus on what I know to be true. A husband and a family that I love. A country that I honor. A God that I worship and obey. Add to that the freedom to have it all.

I love music. I love to ride in my car with the windows down. I love to turn up my radio and sing along with all the songs I adore. When the music turns to songs of "Home" and "Lost," well, I smile and say, "Where have you been all my life, Michael Buble?"

Chapter Twenty

DEAR MOTHER, REMEMBER THE TIME YOU SAID YOU WANTED TO GO TO SLEEP ONE NIGHT AND WAKE UP IN HEAVEN?

I THOUGHT YOU WERE JUST KIDDING.

Seriously, Mother? Couldn't you have left a note or something?

"Dear Regina, Remember the time I said I wanted to go to sleep one night and wake up in heaven? I really wasn't kidding."

Couldn't you have given me some warning?

I know I always wanted that for you. Just not yet. I always prayed God would take you that way. Just not yet. You weren't even sick, for crying out loud. You hadn't spent time in the hospital. No broken bones. Not even a cold. True, your eyes weren't doing well. The doc even mentioned surgery. Blindness lurked about in the not too distant future. You never would have mentally survived that. So I prayed God would take you before that happened. Just not yet. Suffering as Daddy did wouldn't have been good, either. The indignation of wearing diapers, not being able to feed or help yourself in any way, would have secured a room for you in a mental institution. I knew this. So I prayed God would take you. That He'd never allow that to happen. Just not yet.

Remember all the fun times we had this past summer? You said you couldn't get over how much the grandkids had grown. You hardly recognized them. They really surprised you, didn't they? You even went outside to watch them all swim during their visit. You hadn't sat by the pool in the longest time.

Remember this past July 23rd? Your 98th birthday? The sixteen-layer cake? Remember how much fun we had? I never suspected that in less than two months you wouldn't be here any longer. None of us did. We never imagined that this would be the last birthday we'd celebrate with you. The last sixteen-layer birthday cake. The last pictures we'd take together.

Eight years ago, when you decided to move in with us, I

knew how hard you struggled to come to that decision. You never liked Texas. But after a while, you settled in. I think. I hope.

As the years passed, I seemed to have less and less time to sit and chat with you. I'm so sorry about that. The times I hurried about doing what, exactly? Rushing to get you to the end of your sentences. For what reason? It's not like I had an appointment to solve the world's ills. I don't remember being elected Queen. Self-centeredness is all I can offer up.

We never did have a super close relationship, did we? Let's face it, I tended to be a bit rebellious. You were no angel yourself. Your mouth could spit daggers into the next county. Not that it matters now, I suppose. Suffice it to say, we both had our moments of getting on each other's last nerve. Families get to see the ugly in each other that outsiders don't, I guess.

I know there were times I played the *Rain Man* scene in my mind. You know the one where the guy is driving his autistic brother across country and has finally had enough, pulls the car over, walks out into a field, and screams at the top of his lungs. You would have washed my mouth out with soap if I ever used those words. But believe me, I came close. You probably did, too.

I never saw this coming, Mother. That's what haunts me. Should I have? Should I have been more attentive, more intuitive, or even more proactive? Could I have stopped this? Do I honestly think I'm that powerful? Obviously so. I prayed for you to fall asleep one night and wake up in heaven. But when God said, "Yes. This is the perfect time," all I could say was, "Wait! Not yet."

You were happy here weren't you? We made you comfortable didn't we? Life was good, right? I hope so. I know we all tried. But you were winding down. I could see that things were changing for you. Your thought process had slowed. You no longer saw the goodness humans can sometimes exhibit. Food no longer appealed to you. Oh, but you still loved the Atlanta Braves. You drove me crazy talking baseball. I know you did it just to irritate me because you knew I so didn't care. Still, it made us both laugh.

When I asked God to be kind to you, to never let you linger past the time of dignity, I wonder if He understood that I really wanted to have the last say as to when? Of course, you were more ready for it than I. You even said it. Remember? You said, "If I were to die tonight, there's nothing you can do it stop it." Why would you even say that? I never said I could stop it. I only wanted to pick the time. I think I just heard God laugh.

Dinnertime isn't the same, you know. I'm usually okay until dinnertime. I don't know why. You hated most of what I cooked. Always bringing Grandma into it. Who the heck could compete with Grandma when it came to cooking, I ask you? I think I just miss your presence, even as annoyed as I got with your complaints about the food. Every now and then I did actually hit a home run. How's that for a baseball term? Thanksgiving is going to be hard.

I cleaned out your room. Could you have had any more shoes? And pocketbooks? And sunglasses? I always knew you hid snacks in there. You never fooled me for a second. The drawers are all empty now, except for your scarves and the hankie that you've had since I was a little girl. I think I'll keep those. The closet will be home to a few special pieces. I don't have the heart to part with them. You hung up your pink fuzzy housecoat on the back of the door. You tied the sash making sure it looked just so. You never did that before. Did you know you were going away? I left it there. It still has your smell.

I'm not sure when I'll stop wondering when exactly, the

Lord touched your soul, taking you with Him to heaven. I'm not sure when I'll stop feeling so abandoned and orphaned by you and Daddy. Is that just something an only child goes through? I'm sorry I wasn't there to say goodbye.

You outlived your entire birth family. Outlived all but one friend. It seemed to always perplex you as to why the Lord allowed you to live so long. I always thought it was to make sure I stayed in line. We thought so differently about so many things. Like your constant witnessing would have ever made a difference. Okay, so it did. Sometimes. You got that witnessing trait from your father. The eternal God's witness. I believe that between the two of you, you would have witnessed to a tree stump then stood back to watch its rebirth into a giant shade tree. All the cousins used to say that when Papa died and went to heaven he'd probably witness to the Lord.

I want you to know that I tried my best to make sure your funeral happened the way you wanted. *No public viewing* you wrote—underlined three times with three exclamation points (!!!). *My family only*, you wrote. You'll be happy to know that I found Dr. Price. He remembered you and the trip you took together to the Holy Land. Your "spunkiness," as he put it, was what he remembered most. His eulogy would have made you proud. Maryanne did a wonderful job playing the piano. She knew all the songs you asked for. I'm sorry I couldn't get Dr. Hill to sing. But I did get the Minister of Music from your church. You would have loved him. Everyone said it was a beautiful service. I hope so.

There were so many things we'd yet to do together. I'm a little miffed about that I must admit. The trip at Christmas you were looking so forward to. Remember? You really wanted the family in Atlanta to meet our newest member—our sweet Haylie.

In fact you talked about it every day. This wasn't the way to go about making sure they saw her you know. Christmas would have come soon enough, don't you think? I wish we could have made that trip together. Unfinished business really sucks.

So now what? I vacuumed your room again today. I don't know why. It's not like there's anything on the floor to clean up. My mind can't rid itself of the scene of you in your chair. I'll always recall it as that morning when you didn't come down for breakfast. I stood there calling your name over and over again, but you didn't answer. When I touched your leg, I found it cold. My mind knew that the Lord had come in the early morning hours to take you home with Him. Yet, my heart was in disbelief.

You had the most peaceful look on your face. Did you reach for God's hand? Did you feel His grace as He lifted you up into the heavens? Were you frightened? I doubt it. Only because I've known for a long time you were prepared.

I thought I was, too.

I was wrong.

Love,
Regina
Sept. 2014

Postscript

When my mother passed away, naturally my emotions took over. After all the craziness that comes with planning a funeral or the taking care of afterlife necessities, I needed to write her this letter. I'm quite sure Mother would have laughed and said, "Regina, you have always been crazy. But I've always loved you. Even when you thought I didn't." To that, I most likely would have said, "Ditto."

So, I leave you with these passages of scripture that speaks directly to the loss of a loved one.

"Then I heard a voice from heaven say, "Write this: Blessed are the dead who die in the Lord from now on." "Yes," says the Spirit, "they will rest from their labor, for their deeds will follow them." Revelation 14:13

"'He will wipe every tear from their eyes. There will be no more death' or mourning or crying or pain, for the old order of things has passed away.'" Revelation 21:4

"So with you: Now is your time of grief, but I will see you again and you will rejoice, and no one will take away your joy." John 16:22

Epilogue

Dear Friend:

I end with this letter to my mother as a reminder of how God's Word speaks to us in every facet of life, be it public or private. The Bible guides us through everyday occurrences as written about in my award-winning book of short stories entitled,

Anyone Seen My Rose-colored Glasses?
(God's Word in Everyday Life)

God's Word speaks to worldly occurrences. Secular or spiritual topics. God's Word never changes. Its message is ever relevant. This is the purpose of this book.

A Place Called Common Sense (God's Word in a Secular World)

For the Lord grants wisdom!
From his mouth come knowledge and understanding.
He grants a treasure of **common sense** to the honest.
He is a shield to those who walk with integrity.
He guards the paths of the just
and protects those who are faithful to him.
Then you will understand what is right, just, and fair,
and you will find the right way to go.
For wisdom will enter your heart,
and knowledge will fill you with joy.
Wise choices will watch over you.
Understanding will keep you safe.
Wisdom will save you from evil people,
from those whose words are twisted.
Proverbs 2:7-12

A PLACE CALLED *Common Sense*

I hope I've touched your heart in some way and taken you on a journey to a place called common sense. I hope I've stirred your senses and made you think or even reconsider a few things. Maybe look at things a little more differently. I hope I've even made you chuckle a time or two.

Most of all, I hope you find peace and comfort in God's Word—a place called common sense.

To God be the glory.

May you be richly blessed by His loving grace.

And,

His Word.

www.ingramcontent.com/pod-product-compliance
Lightning Source LLC
LaVergne TN
LVHW090115080426
835507LV00040B/899